Also by O. S. Hawkins

When Revival Comes

After Revival Comes

Clues to a Successful Life

Where Angels Fear to Tread

Tracing the Rainbow through the Rain

*Unmasked! . . . Recognizing and Dealing with Imposters
in the Church*

Getting Down to Brass Tacks

MEETING THE GOD OF
THE SECOND CHANCE

JONAH

O.S. HAWKINS

LOIZEAUX BROTHERS
Neptune, New Jersey

Printed in the United States of America.
A Publication of Loizeaux Brothers, Inc.
A Nonprofit Organization Devoted to the Lord's Work
and to the Spread of His Truth.

Scripture quotations in this book are from the
New International Version of the Bible.

Library of Congress Cataloging-in-Publication Data

Hawkins, O. S.,
Jonah: meeting the God of the second chance / O. S. Hawkins.
Includes bibliographical references.
ISBN 0-87213-323-0
1. Bible.   O.T. Jonah—Commentaries.   I. Title.
BS1605.3.H37   1990
224'.9207—dc20   89-77398

10   9   8   7   6   5   4   3   2

To Holly

When I first laid eyes on her the moment she was born,
the Holy Spirit began to pray through me
the words of a great hymn:

How sweet to hold a new born baby
And feel the pride and joy she gives
But greater still the calm assurance
This child can face uncertain days
Because He lives!

She is everything a dad could ever want in a daughter
and she is as much like Jesus as anyone I know.
I am very proud to be her dad.

CONTENTS

ACKNOWLEDGMENTS

I am indebted to a number of people who, in their own unique and diversified ways, have made this volume a reality:

My friends at Loizeaux . . . I am so proud to be on their "team." They have not strayed from their roots or purpose in over one hundred years of publishing.

Susie, Wendy, and Holly . . . my wife and daughters who continue to allow me time to study and write. As God has enlarged our personal ministry, they have never once complained about sharing me with others.

Wanda Todd . . . my administrative assistant. This volume, like those before, would not be a reality without her tireless efforts.

The fellowship of believers . . . at the First Baptist Church in Fort Lauderdale, Florida. They are on their way to "Nineveh" and are anticipating a mighty revival!

Dr. R. T. Kendall . . . minister at the Westminster Chapel in London and "bone fisherman" par excellence. Any serious study on Jonah will include his classic volume, *Jonah*. While fishing and fellowshipping together we have talked much about Jonah's pilgrimage. Many of my thoughts took form while sitting in a boat on the flats of the Florida Keys and in Bimini. I have come to conclude, with Kendall, that in the end Jonah came through. As R.T. put it, "He let God have the last word!"

MEETING THE GOD OF
THE SECOND CHANCE

JONAH

O.S. HAWKINS

INTRODUCTION

I. THE STORY OF A MAN'S PILGRIMAGE
   A. Rejection
   B. Reflection
   C. Correction
   D. Objection

II. THE STORY OF GOD'S PROVIDENCE
   A. Election
   B. Protection
   C. Perfection
   D. Affection

Novels. Short stories. So many excellent works of fiction are waiting to be discovered in our city and church libraries. Who could forget the pathos of Ernest Hemingway's *Old Man and the Sea*? I am pleased to have come upon the writings of Jeffrey Archer of England. His *Quiver Full of Arrows* is one of the finest collections of short stories ever written. But the little book of Jonah tucked away in the Old Testament has them all beat. It is filled with suspense, drama, lessons for life—and it really happened. It is not fiction.

Although Jonah is one of the most popular books in the Bible, it is also one of the most controversial. Its historical validity is questioned by skeptics and scholars alike. Jonah is the story of a man who rebelled and then was swallowed by a great fish. Why should we think it strange that God could prepare a fish to swallow Jonah? If you were in my city today, I would take you to Port Everglades. Docked in that port, you would find a nuclear submarine, a great vessel of human ingenuity and engineering that can keep persons alive for several months under the sea. If human beings can prepare an iron fish like that, why do some of us have difficulty believing that the God who made the world and flung the stars in space could perform a miracle as mundane as preparing a fish for a runaway prophet named Jonah?

But the book of Jonah is not about a fish; in fact, only three verses deal with the fish. The other forty-five verses tell us the real message of Jonah's story. It is the story of someone like you and me. It is the story of his struggles, calling, disobedience, problems, and prayer life. It is the story of his second chance, his successes and failures.

The book of Jonah is a book about Jesus. Jesus? In the Old Testament? Yes. In fact, our Lord himself said:

> A wicked and adulterous generation asks for a miraculous sign! But none will be given it except the sign of the prophet Jonah. For as Jonah was three days and three nights in the belly of a huge fish, so the Son of Man will be three days and three nights in the heart of the earth. The men of Nineveh will stand up at the judgment with this generation and condemn it; for they repented at the preaching of Jonah, and now one greater than Jonah is here (Matthew 12:39-41).

The late G. Campbell Morgan, formerly pastor of Westminster Chapel in London, said, "Men have been looking so long at the great fish they have failed to see the great God!" In this present book that is what we want to avoid. We want to see this great God and follow his will.

Perhaps no other book in the Bible is as ridiculed as this one. There are at least three basic ways in which the book can be understood. Some view it as an allegory, a long story with a hidden meaning. Those who see it allegorically equate each major character to some event of historical significance. For example, they might see it as an allegory of the Babylonian captivity. In that view, Jonah is Israel, Nineveh is pagan idolatry, the sea is world politics, the ship is diplomacy, the storm is the Babylonian overthrow of Assyria, Jonah inside the fish is the Babylonian exile, and Jonah's deliverance is the return from exile. Others who see it allegorically see it as the church during the persecution and its deliverance when Jesus returns.[1]

Others approach this book as though it were a parable; that is, it did not happen historically. Rather, it is a cleverly written short story dating to the postexilic period. It is a parable with one main point: the deliverance of Israel. If, however, Jonah is to be treated as a parable, then it is certainly found in strange company, being in the midst of all the other historical prophetic books.

Then there are those like myself who hold to the literal historical approach. That is to say, there really was a man named Jonah, who was actually swallowed by a fish. We do know that Jonah was a figure of history. Second Kings 14:25 gives his further historical significance: "He was the one who restored the boundaries of Israel from Lebo Hamath to the Sea of the Arabah, in accordance with the word of the Lord, the God of Israel, spoken through his servant Jonah son of Amittai, the prophet from Gath Hepher."

One characteristic of a parable in the Bible is that a person's name is never mentioned. For example, there is the parable of the prodigal son. We do not know his name, nor his father's, nor his older brother's name. There we have an indication that Jonah, the main character, was not parabolic, but a literal and historical figure.

The main reason I believe in a literal Jonah is that our Lord Jesus obviously believed in his historicity. Therefore, when people question the historicity of Jonah, in reality they are questioning the integrity of the Lord Jesus Christ. Our Lord related Jonah to his own resurrection; and if Jonah's experience was not historical, such an association would not have made sense.

Those who discount the authenticity of Jonah are subtly undermining the deity and integrity of our Lord Jesus Christ. Was He deceitful? Did Jesus tell us a lie when He said that Jonah was in a fish's belly three days and three nights? Of course He didn't. Was He deceived? Did Jesus actually think that Jonah was an allegory or a parable? Of course not. He is "the Truth." Our confidence in the word of God doesn't allow us to take from its historicity simply because something is miraculous.

In effect, Jesus was saying that Jonah was *a sign* that prophesied his own death and resurrection (Matthew 12:39-41). Think about that. Is it any wonder that the book of Jonah then is one of the most openly attacked books in the Bible? You see, if the story of Jonah is fiction, so is the gospel. Jesus said, "For as Jonah was . . . so the Son of Man will be. . . ." If the book of Jonah is not true, what confidence can we have in Matthew, Mark, Luke, or John being true? Here is a test of true orthodoxy. If you want to know whether a man or woman is orthodox or not, ask them their opinion of Jonah. If they deny the historical authenticity of Jonah, I suspect that they will also deny the authenticity of the resurrection of the Lord Jesus Christ. Any time someone says it doesn't matter whether this book is historical or not, don't you believe it. It does matter. We are dealing here with a real man who lived in and around 800 B.C. and whose message is as relevant today as the morning newspaper.

What is the message of Jonah? I believe that this book gives us tremendous insights into our relationship with the Lord Jesus Christ. It is the story of a man's pilgrimage and God's providence.

I. THE STORY OF A MAN'S PILGRIMAGE

A. Rejection

We can write across the first chapter of Jonah the word *rejection*. In chapter 1 God called Jonah to go to Nineveh and be the agent of revival. But Jonah went in the opposite direction, choosing to reject the will of God for his life. He went down to the seaport town of Joppa and boarded a ship sailing for Tarshish.

How do *you* relate to the will of God? Jonah was afraid of God's will, so he ran. Many people find themselves living in chapter 1 of Jonah—that is, rejecting the will of God for their lives.

B. Reflection

Across chapter 2 we can write the word *reflection*. There in the belly of the fish Jonah began to reflect. He prayed and praised God. The fish eventually regurgitated him up on shore.

This is where many people live today. Some people have to go down, down, down, before they surrender to God's will. Often the adversities of life bring us to this moment of reflection.

C. Correction

Across chapter 3 we can write the word *correction*. As he sat on the shore "the word of the Lord came to Jonah a second time." He got up, obeyed the word of God, went to Nineveh, and a mighty revival ensued. Yes, God is the God of the second chance. Jonah corrected his ways.

There is a tragic truth here. Warren Weirsbe is correct in observing that it took God longer to prepare his servant and get him to obey his call than it did for the entire godless city of Nineveh to repent. Things haven't changed much, have they? It still takes God longer to get Christians right than it does to get sinners to repent.

I'm so glad that God is the God of a second chance. If I did not believe that human beings could be made whole, if I did not believe that the gospel was a gospel of the second chance, I would never preach or write again.

D. Objection

Across chapter 4 we can write the word *objection*. One would think that Jonah's heart would have leaped for joy when revival came to Nineveh. There he was in the will of God, used by God in a mighty way. But no. He was angry that God sent revival. He wanted God to destroy the city. He objected to the fact that God poured out revival on heathen Nineveh.

Jonah laid bare his soul for us here. If we had written the book, most of us would have ended it at Jonah 3:10, with the account of the great revival. But Jonah went on and added the fourth chapter to show us his shortcomings and how prone we all are to this spirit of objection. Some of us live here in chapter 4. We get in the will of God and are being used by God, and then He does something and we object to it. God blesses someone else, and we get jealous.

We already see that Jonah is far more than the story of a man and a fish. It is the story of a man's pilgrimage, but it is more than that.

II. THE STORY OF GOD'S PROVIDENCE

The purpose of the word of God is to reveal the God of the word. This too we see in Jonah: the beautiful story of God's providence.

A. Election

Looking from God's point of view, we can write across chapter 1 the word *election*. One cannot read the first chapter of Jonah without seeing the sovereignty of God. God chose Jonah. God called Jonah. God is in control. Can you see him here? God controlled the ship. God controlled the wind. God controlled the sailors' dice. God controlled the waves. God controlled the fish.

God elects his own people, assigns their duties, appoints their places. He calls particular people to particular places for particular purposes. In this case, He called Jonah to Nineveh for revival. What a wonderful picture we see of our Lord here. He is concerned for you. He calls *you*. And the truth is that you cannot run from him.

B. Protection

Across chapter 2 we can write the word *protection*. God protected his man even when he was in rebellion. He "prepared" a great fish to consume Jonah and keep him from drowning.

Here too we see a picture of our Lord Jesus. When we go our own ways in willful disobedience, He continues to pursue us. Even in our rebellion He protects us until we come to ourselves. The very thing that some people are lamenting today—their mishaps in life—just may be a giant fish that God has prepared to protect them from themselves and their rebellion.

C. Perfection

Across chapter 3, from God's point of view, we can write the word *perfection*. The Bible says that God perfects what concerns us. The Bible admonishes us not to be conformed to the world but to be transformed that we might prove what is that "good, and acceptable, and *perfect* will of God" (Romans 12:2 KJV).

In chapter 3 God sent a mighty revival. God's will was finally done. When we obey his will and share his word, we can see his blessing. The psalmist said, "Will you not revive us again, that your people may rejoice in you?" God is more interested in revival than we are. He is about the business of perfecting all things that concern us. What a picture we see of our Lord Jesus also here in chapter 3. He is just waiting to send revival. His problem is that it takes him longer to get us ready than it does for whole cities to repent.

D. Affection

Across chapter 4 we can write the word *affection*. Here God taught Jonah a lesson. Jonah was ecstatic about the vine that God had sent, and then God sent the little worm. Sometimes we get our eyes fixed on lesser things, when the main thing is to keep the main thing always the main thing. What a wonderful picture we see of our Lord here too as He appealed to Jonah by saying, "Nineveh has more than a hundred and twenty thousand people who cannot tell their right hand from their left, and many cattle as well. Should I not be concerned about that great city?" (4:11).

God has compassion for sinners. His heart beats with concern for the lost and ungodly. We may shun them but our Lord Jesus doesn't. He has compassion and affection for those in need of salvation.

A lot of boats are sailing for Tarshish today. But the red flag of warning is that a storm is raging on that route. Perhaps you already have been quickened by the fact that God has called you to Nineveh and you are thinking about going down to Joppa and finding a boat to Tarshish. The way to Nineveh is the way of revival. The way of Tarshish is the way to ruin.

For those who sail for Tarshish, we read that the word came to Jonah "a second time" (3:1). What good news. God is the God of the second chance. Moses broke the tablets of the law, but God gave his law to him a second time. Samson sinned, but God gave him a second chance. Peter cursed the Lord, who then met him on the shore and gave him a second chance.

Some people have written across their lives the word *rejection*. Perhaps this chapter has brought some readers to the word *reflection*. The intent of this devotional volume is to move us all to the word *correction*, that we might know the will of God for our lives and do it.

---

1. Huffman, John A. Jr. 1985. "Running Away from God." (Printed Sermon, p. 2).

CHAPTER ONE
Here Am I . . . Send Someone Else
Jonah 1:1-3

I. JONAH'S CALL
    A. Personal
    B. Pointed
    C. Purposeful

II. JONAH'S FALL
    A. Calculated
    B. Continuous
    C. Costly

God calls particular people to particular places for particular purposes. In Jonah's case, we find God calling him to Nineveh to preach against its sin. But when God called Jonah, he replied, "Here am I . . . send someone else. I'm on my way to Tarshish!"

What a contrast that response was to the call of the prophet Isaiah. When God asked, "Whom shall I send? And who will go for us?" Isaiah's response was, "Here am I. Send me!"

Many Christians today are like Jonah. It may be that Nineveh for some of us is reconciliation. The Nineveh to which God calls others may be repentance. Still others may be called to the Nineveh of restitution.

A lot of us are on boats that are sailing for Tarshish while God is saying, "Go to Nineveh." Where are you headed? There are really only two roads in the Christian life. One leads to Nineveh, the other to Tarshish. One road is the will of God; the other is disobedience to his will.

Somewhere there is a job for you that no one else can do quite the way you can do it. Each of us is indescribably valuable to God. Each of us has a special part in the body of Christ. No one is unimportant.

I. JONAH'S CALL

The word of the Lord came to Jonah son of Amittai: "Go to the great city of Nineveh and preach against it, because its wickedness has come up before me" (Jonah 1:1-2).

A. Personal

The call of the Lord is personal. Jonah was a real person who lived in a real city just like you and I, and God called him for a special task. The Bible says, "The word of the Lord came to Jonah son of Amittai." It was a personal call. It was "to Jonah." God did not call Habakkuk nor Amos nor Obadiah, nor any of the other prophets to go to Nineveh.

This was not the word of man; it was "the word of the Lord." Men do not call us; it is God who calls us. Jonah had a God who spoke to him.

I don't know how God talked to Jonah. He did not have the word of God, the final complete written revelation, as we do today. Perhaps God spoke to him audibly, as He did to Abraham. Perhaps God spoke to him in a vision, as He did with Peter on the rooftop or with Ezekiel. Or maybe it was in a dream, as it was with Joseph. It may simply have been an impression on his heart. How He spoke to him is not important. What is important is that the word of the Lord got through to a human being.

God still speaks to his servants today, and his call is just as personal.

We have a God who speaks to our hearts in a still, small voice. It is strange how it never occurs to some believers that the same God who spoke to the prophets in the past now speaks to us directly by the Holy Spirit through his word. Some people have no difficulty whatsoever believing that God spoke to this man Jonah, but that God would speak to them is extremely difficult to believe.

Has the word of the Lord come to you this week? If not, you have not spent time with him. God still speaks to us personally. The writer of Hebrews put it like this, "In the past God spoke to our forefathers through the prophets at many times and in various ways, but in these last days he has spoken to us by his Son, whom he appointed heir of all things, and through whom he made the universe" (Hebrews 1:1-2). What are we doing about the fact that God speaks to us personally? It is no wonder that later in Hebrews we read, "Today, if you hear his voice do not harden your hearts" (Hebrews 3:7-8).

I remember a Friday evening all-night bus ride from Matamoros, Mexico, to Fort Worth, Texas. I was a college pre-law student but that night on that bus God spoke to me and called me into the ministry. I cannot explain it but I know He did it. It could not have been more real had He been seated beside me physically on that bus. God spoke to my heart and called me to preach and I've known from that moment that I could not find happiness in a court of law or in doing anything else. God still calls particular people to particular places for particular purposes—and not just preachers. He calls teachers and lawyers and business people and housewives and bank tellers and scientists, if we would but listen. David said that God makes known to us the path of life, and in his presence is fullness of joy (Psalm 16:11). And a good thing to remember is that God doesn't call the equipped; He equips the called.

The Gold Coast of Florida, including the greater Fort Lauderdale-Miami area, has become one of the large metropolitan areas of the world, with over three million people now residing in this beautiful tropical paradise. A lot of people come to our city to get lost in the teeming masses. It is easy to become nameless here. No one knows you. No one is watching you.

But we all need to remember that God knows us. God knows our names, addresses, and telephone numbers. He knows our backgrounds, our parents, and brothers and sisters. Even before we were formed in the womb, He said, "I knew you, before you were born I set you apart" (Jeremiah 1:5). The beautiful thing about life in Christ is that He gives purpose and personhood. God calls us personally to himself. It is a happy day in the life of any believer when he or she comes to realize that the Lord Jesus is interested in them personally: at school, on the ballfield, at the office, in the home, at the grocery store, struggling with the finances, in good times and in bad times.

B. Pointed

The call of the Lord is pointed. God said, "Go to Nineveh." It was a clear call. It was pointed. It was urgent. God did not tell Jonah to go to Jerusalem or Shechem, or Joppa, or anywhere else. His call was to Nineveh, a city founded by Nimrod shortly after the confusion of tongues at the tower of Babel.

Nineveh was a great city in what is modernday Iraq. Its streets were twenty miles long and its walls one hundred feet high. The walls around Nineveh were so wide that three chariots could be driven abreast across the top of them. Historians believe that the population exceeded hundreds of thousands; the Bible tells us that one hundred and twenty thousand did not know their right hand from their left (perhaps a description of small children). It was a city of great wickedness and it was the capital of Assyria.

Why would God call Jonah to go to Nineveh, when Nineveh was a gentile city, and God was working with the Jews? Surely Nineveh was not on Jonah's preaching schedule. We don't know why God picks certain places. For example, why were you born where you were born and not in another country or century with different parents? I was born on August 16, 1947, in Fort Worth, Texas. It would have made a profound difference in my life had I been born three years earlier in Hiroshima or Nagasaki.

Like other Israelites, Jonah believed that God blessed his people in two ways: first, by directly blessing Israel spiritually and temporally; and second, by sending adversities on their enemies. Thus, a famine in Nineveh would be considered a blessing to Israel. Things haven't changed much, have they? Many of us feel as if someone's victory is a defeat for ourselves. And some people even believe that someone else's downfall in some way lifts them up. A call to go to Nineveh went against the grain of a Jewish prophet like Jonah. In fact, a comforting hope Israel held to was the hope that some day God would pour out wrath on Nineveh. Now, instead of that, God was calling Jonah to go and preach to them the message of salvation. It seems that even in Old Testament times our Lord was giving us a glimpse of what He would one day say on a Galilean hillside: "Love your enemies and pray for those who persecute you" (Matthew 5:44).

Those ancient Jews had it in their minds that God loved them and them alone. What a surprise Jonah must have felt when he received word from God to "go to the great city of Nineveh." Had God commanded him to go to Jerusalem or Bethlehem or some other city, it might have been different. But Nineveh? A pagan city?

Before we are quick to point a finger of accusation, however, we must understand that in some ways we are no better than Jonah. We too can get to thinking that God loves us more than He does others. We live in America, a so-called Christian nation. We are the so-called "people of God." When we read that God called Jonah to go to Nineveh, it ought to remind us of our commission to take the gospel to the entire world. This pointed call smacks in the face of any exclusivism or cliquishness on our part. Can you sense its missionary spirit?

God loves the Soviets, the Iranians, the Lebanese, the Syrians, the Israelis, the Palestinians. The Bible says, "For God so loved the *world* that he gave his one and only Son."

C. Purposeful

God's call is purposeful. God instructed Jonah to go to Nineveh and "preach against it, because its wickedness has come up before me." The Lord is never vague in his call. Jonah was to cry out against the wickedness of Nineveh. What a task God assigned him. He would be one lonely voice in the midst of that city, calling its people to revival and repentance. Think about that. What could one man do?

The verbs in verse 2 are imperatives. They are commands. Go. Preach.[1] God's calling is not merely one of several options if we intend to be in his will. Some people hear the call of God to a particular place for a particular purpose and they think, "Well, I'll decide about that later." We all need to be reminded that God's calling is always in the imperative. Jonah was not to be concerned with success. He was simply to obey the call. Jonah was not to go and preach philosophy. He was not to go and speak religious platitudes. He was not to go and address social issues. He was not to go and set up a blood bank and begin a clothing ministry. He was to "preach against their sin." Surely God is calling more people to this task today than are evidently on the scene. The twentieth-century cruise business to Tarshish must be booming in the church of the Lord Jesus Christ. Where are the prophets who, as Joel said, "weep between the temple porch and the altar" (Joel 2:17) over the sins of the people?

Thank God for those in our own nation who are standing against the humanistic philosophy that has subtly infiltrated our culture. This cancer is especially preying on young minds in the public schools. It is no wonder the humanists are so determined in their effort to keep prayer out of public schools. They want no acknowledgment of God, so there will be no sense of sin, which is the breaking of his commandments.

Today four men are ruling America from their graves. Charles Darwin tells us that sin is just a hangover from our animalistic background. John Dewey, the leading promoter of pragmatism, tells us that human beings can be educated out of what drags them down. He says that sin is not our problem; a lack of education is. Sigmund Freud tells us that the concept of sin is what is wrong with people in the first place. Karl Marx tells us that man's problem is basically economic; put him in the right economic state and he will prosper. Those four philosophies are ruling America. But where are those standing between the porch and the altar, crying out against the wickedness of our day?

Whatever became of sin? Man's problem is not fundamentally biological nor educational nor psychological nor economical. Man's problem is sin, rebellion.

To cry out against the wickedness of our day is not easy. Why? Mainly because we cannot cry out against the sins of others with sin in our own hearts and lives. Could this be the reason so few Christians are really standing against the tide of sin today? It is difficult to speak out against pornography if you yourself subscribe to certain magazines and read illicit literature in airports when no one is looking. It is difficult to cry out against prostitution if you personally think nothing of having extramarital affairs. It is difficult to speak out against marijuana if you smoke cigars and cigarettes. It is a difficult thing to speak out against dope if you are a social drinker. It is difficult to speak against X-rated movie enterprises if you are glued to television soap operas with all their adultery and fornication. In such an environment, is it any wonder that many of God's people are enroute to Tarshish today? God calls us to a purpose, and that purpose is to cry out against the wickedness around us.

II. JONAH'S FALL

But Jonah ran away from the Lord and headed for Tarshish. He went down to Joppa, where he found a ship bound for that port. After paying the fare, he went aboard and sailed for Tarshish to flee from the Lord (Jonah 1:3).

A. Calculated

Jonah's fall from the Lord was calculated. What an honor had come to him. God chose him to go to Nineveh with the message of revival. Jonah must have been the most humbled and challenged man in all the land.

Jonah 1:3 begins with two words that may be the saddest words in the whole book, "But Jonah." Instead of being thankful, Jonah fled from God's will. He was not different from us. So many of us have doubted God's word. Remember, Jonah was a prophet called of God. He knew the Lord, and knew that the Lord had called him. I dare say there are those reading this volume who know the Lord, who have been called by the Lord, and perhaps like Jonah have fled from the will of God. Perhaps you are a young man whom God is calling into the ministry, but you are enroute to Tarshish. Perhaps you are a young woman reading these words while living in sin, knowing that her Nineveh is repentance.

The Bible tells us that he went down to Joppa. He found a ship. He bought a ticket. This was no passing whim. This was a calculated decision.

When we fall from the Lord, it is always calculated. We make plans to do wrong and we follow them through. Tarshish was the farthest known city of that day. It is believed to have been in Spain, over two thousand miles from Joppa. When people leave God, they always go as far away as they can. Remember the story Jesus told of the prodigal son who went to the "far country" when he left the will of his father. Tarshish was as far west as one could go. Nineveh was to the east.

A lot of us have a Tarshish out there somewhere. It's that place where we think we can minister as effectively as we could at Nineveh. But remember, when we go to Tarshish and God has called us to Nineveh, we go without his blessing.

When we really think about it, this is incredible. Here was God's man. Why would he run away from *life*? Perhaps it was because of fear of the unknown. Think about it. What if God called you to go to Tehran (Iran) today? The people are so different. The culture is so opposite from ours and so antagonistic toward us. A lot of us might be running to Tarshish because of the unknown.

Perhaps Jonah went to Tarshish because he was afraid he would become unpopular. I suppose a lot of people are running away from the will of God for fear of being unpopular.

It could have been that he left God's will because he was unconcerned. It might be that he was just not concerned that Nineveh come to repentance. After all, he held some animosity toward them. He knew all about the people of Nineveh and had witnessed their cruelty and brutality. They were known for their savagery. They burned children alive and tortured adults by skinning them and leaving them to die in the scorching sun.[2] Is it any wonder he went to Tarshish?

It is not unusual for modernday Jonahs to want to run from difficult things. A lot of people are on the run today simply because they don't want to face difficult tasks. It is easier to get a divorce than it is to go to Nineveh and be in the will of God. So many think the route to Tarshish is so much easier . . . until they are on board ship.

The real reason Jonah fled is found in the first verses of chapter 4 of this book: "But Jonah was greatly displeased and became angry. He prayed to the Lord, 'O Lord, is this not what I said when I was still at home? This is why I was so quick to flee to Tarshish. I knew that you are a gracious and compassionate God, slow to anger and abounding in love, a God who relents from sending calamity'" (Jonah 4:1-2). Jonah could not believe that God would shower his grace on the gentiles, especially those who had been so ruthless with the Jews. Jonah wanted no part of that. We see a lot of the same spirit in the prodigal's brother who "became angry and refused to go in" when his wayward brother returned (Luke 15:28).

So Jonah ran from the presence of the Lord. Jonah's fall was a calculated fall. He knew where he was going, and he was going his own way. "He was running away from the Lord" (1:10). When we are on the run, we forget the truths of scripture. Probably Jonah had read a thousand times the words of the psalmist:

> Where can I go from your Spirit?
>   Where can I flee from your presence?
> If I go up to the heavens, you are there;
>   if I make my bed in the depths, you are there.
> If I rise on the wings of the dawn,
>   if I settle on the far side of the sea,
> even there your hand will guide me,
>   your right hand will hold me fast
>   (Psalm 139:7-10).

Jonah thought he could flee from the presence of the Lord. He knew better, but his sin had blinded him to the truth of scripture. This happens to people when they are on the run from the will of God. They find themselves doing things they know better than to do. We forget what we know when we are on the run from God.

Jonah wasn't the first nor the last person in the Bible who tried to flee from the presence of the Lord. Adam and Eve tried to flee from God's presence. Like Jonah, they disobeyed, and God came to mend the broken relationship. But the first thing they did was try to hide. "The man and his wife heard the sound of the Lord God as he was walking in the garden in the cool of the day, and they hid from the Lord God among the trees of the garden" (Genesis 3:8). It was the same with Cain after he killed his brother Abel. He deliberately rebelled and the Bible says, "So Cain went out from the Lord's presence and lived in the land of Nod, east of Eden" (Genesis 4:16). On and on we could go throughout the Bible. And it is the same with so many people today. In our rebellion, we think we can hide from the Lord—but we can't.

Don't be so foolish as to think you can flee from God's presence. God said, "Can anyone hide in secret places so that I cannot see him? . . . Do not I fill heaven and earth?" (Jeremiah 23:24). We cannot run away from God. It is a tragic mistake to think we can.

It is interesting that the Bible says he "found a ship." He was looking for it. It is a dangerous thing to try to justify our rebellion simply because things seem to fall in place. Some people think that just because they "find a ship" it must be all right. Someone leaves God for a life of sin and says it must be right; look how everything is turning out. You too may find your ship, and it may sail right on time, but if you are enroute to Tarshish when God has called you to Nineveh, a storm is brewing and sooner or later you are going overboard.

It is amazing how skilled the devil is in his manipulative powers. For example, a woman leaves her husband because she found a ship to Tarshish. Oh, there was someone else who was always there and was so kind and understanding. A man gets himself into legal trouble because he found a ship for Tarshish. He was in a financial bind and thought "just this once." A young Christian woman marries an unsaved man because she found a ship for Tarshish. "Oh, he'll get saved after the wedding," is her wishful thought. The truth is, any time we want to run away from the will of God, one thing is certain. We will find a ship to Tarshish, and the devil will make sure that it is sailing right on time. Satan always sees that transportation is provided for those who are running from the will of God.

B. Continuous

Jonah's fall from the Lord was continuous. Note his ongoing downward digression. He went down to Joppa. He went down into the ship. He went down into the sea. He went down into the fish's belly. He went down into the deep. Here is a vivid picture of a life fleeing from God. It is characterized in the King James Version by these words: down, down, down. There is something eerie about the sound of these words in verses 3 and 5. It is as though an ominous dark storm cloud were gathering and you can see it coming. Then it unloads thunder, lightning, and pelting rain.

Once we step on the pathway of disobedience, the road keeps spiraling downward. David started going down when he watched Bathsheba bathing. He went down farther when he called for her. He went down farther into adultery. He went down farther when he had her husband Uriah killed. He went down farther when he tried to cover over his sin. He kept going down, down, down, until he repented.

Falling from God's will brings on the feeling that we cannot stop. I remember learning to snow ski in the Santa Fe ski basin in New Mexico. On the first day of my first attempt, a friend and I got on the wrong ski lift and went to the top of the mountain instead of to the beginners' slope. The farther down we went, the steeper it got and the faster we went and we couldn't stop until we crashed. This is the way it is in leaving the will of God. When we fall from his will it is not only a calculated fall, but a continuous fall until we crash.

If we could only learn this simple lesson: No one ever goes up while living in rebellion against God. A lot of people today are fooling themselves. A fall is just what it says it is. People never fall up; they fall down. There is no standing still on the way to Tarshish.

C. Costly

Jonah's fall from the Lord was costly. The Bible says that Jonah paid the fare. We pay our own way when we flee from the Lord. Galatians 6:7 says, "Do not be deceived: God cannot be mocked. A man reaps what he sows."

The rest of Jonah's story shows us that the trip was more expensive than he ever dreamed. That is the way it is with sin. The Bible says, "The wages of sin is death" (Romans 6:23). Have you considered the cost of fleeing from the will of the Lord?

As a pastor, I have seen so many who are paying the fare of a life of rebellion against the will of God. I know men who left their family and the will of the Lord and are paying the fare. I know some who are hooked on narcotics and are paying the fare. I visited with a man in prison not long ago who left the will of the Lord and is paying the fare. I see it in the faces of men on the streets of our city who are paying the fare. Yes, the way of the transgressor is hard. The prodigal son out in the far country feeding the swine was paying the fare.

When we fall from God's will it is costly. Ask the woman who married the unsaved man; he was lying when he said he would never leave nor forsake her. Ask the man whom God called into the ministry who instead went to Tarshish. Ask the prostitute at the corner who is forty years old and looks sixty. Ask some of the street people who line up at the clothing ministry of our church. Each one is some mother's son; some of them are somebody's daddy. They are the shadows of the men they might have been. Ask the teenage runaway girls on the Fort Lauderdale strip. I see people paying the price of running from God every day of every week. I see it in the faces of men, women, and young people. I see it in the guilt-ridden faces of singles who think that everybody else is doing it.

The most expensive thing a person does is run from God. It costs some people their jobs, others their families, some their reputations, others joy and peace.

The fall from God's will is a calculated fall, a continuous fall, and a costly fall, until we repent and return to him. When we return to him we hear his clear voice still calling us personally, pointedly, and purposefully.

How wonderful it is to know that Jesus paid our fare for us on Calvary. There He took our sin that we might take his righteousness. He died our death that we might live his life. Yes, "Jesus paid it all, all to him I owe; sin had left a crimson stain, He washed it white as snow."

God still calls people today. However, when God called Jonah he answered, "Here I am . . . send someone else!" Let's be honest. There is a bit of Jonah in all of us. Many of us have heard God's call and have gone the other way, only to find that the fall has been continuous and costly. God still speaks to us today. Despite our rebellion, He stays after us as He did Jonah.

> Let none hear you idly saying
> There is nothing I can do.
> While the souls of men are dying
> And the Master calls for YOU.
> Take the task He gives you gladly
> Let his work your pleasure be;
> Answer quickly while He calleth
> "Here am I, send me, send me."

---

1. Draper, James T., Jr. 1971. *Jonah: Living in Rebellion.* Wheaton IL: Tyndale House Publishers, p.18.
2. Blair, J. Allen. 1963. *Jonah.* Neptune NJ: Loizeaux Brothers, Inc., p. 20.

CHAPTER TWO
Lessons on Leaving the Lord
Jonah 1:3-10

I. ASPIRATIONS
II. OBLIGATIONS
III. COMMUNICATIONS
IV. REPUTATIONS

I had always wanted a camelhair overcoat. Pastoring in the cold icy Oklahoma winters made a camelhair overcoat the common desire of a lot of people. We had just been through one of the coldest winters on record. Merchants in Ada, Oklahoma, always celebrated the end of the winter season with a half-price sale in order to clear their racks and make ready for the spring fashions. So I took the plunge and bought the camelhair overcoat I had always wanted and packed it away securely to await next winter. However, that winter never came. We moved to Fort Lauderdale, Florida, where it is seventy degrees twelve months of the year. After living here a few years (and never wearing the overcoat) I received an invitation to preach in Minneapolis, Minnesota, in the middle of February. I readily accepted, knowing it would be a tremendous opportunity to "break in" my new camelhair overcoat. I rose early on the appointed morning, and laid my overcoat and briefcase near the front door while I said my goodbyes to the family before heading off to the airport. Having checked in for the flight, I was sitting in my seat and the plane was barreling down the runway when a haunting thought came to me: I had left my overcoat by the front door at home. I left it. My big opportunity to wear my new coat—and I blew it! Minneapolis greeted me with a temperature of eight degrees below zero and snow drifts of eight feet. And I greeted Minneapolis without my coat.

Have you ever left anything? It is a terrible feeling. It leaves an emptiness when we leave something that is dear to us. Jonah left something. In fact, he left a lot when he left the Lord. He left his aspirations. I have seen men and women who aspired to do great things for God, but in getting out of his will they left those aspirations when they left him.

Jonah also left his obligations. I have also seen people who have left their obligations. Once they were active in the service of Christ, but today they are asleep in the storm.

Jonah also left his communications. I have seen this in the faces of men and women who once prayed, once had a sweet fellowship with God. But when they left his will for their lives they left the ability to communicate with him.

Jonah also left his reputation. I've seen men and women who once were looked on with respect and appreciation. Once they had a testimony. But when they left the Lord's will, they left their reputations and their testimonies behind.

We often talk about what it costs to serve God, but Jonah gave us a vivid picture of what it costs to leave God.

I. ASPIRATIONS

But Jonah ran away from the Lord and headed for Tarshish. He went down to Joppa, where he found a ship bound for that port. After paying the fare, he went aboard and sailed for Tarshish to flee from the Lord (Jonah 1:3).

Jonah had a calling from God to go to Nineveh. This was God's will for his life. He was a prophet of God, a man of God, and he had aspired to know God's way until he left the will of God.

Then he also left his aspirations behind. He resigned his calling.

Everything in the book of Jonah obeys God's will except his own man. Think about it. God sent the waves and they obeyed. The lots obeyed. The storm obeyed. The fish obeyed. The worm obeyed. Birds fulfill the will of God in their lives. Snakes fulfill the will of God in their lives. Man was made to fellowship with God, and he is the only one of all of God's creations who is not fulfilling his purpose and will.

Some people think they can get out of the will of God and maintain their Christian aspirations at the same time. They are deceived into believing they can go on in their sin, and God's mercy will simply cover them. If we can go on and on in unrepented sin without the chastisement of God, that is certainly not a sign of his mercy. It may be a sign that God is giving us over (as He said in Romans 1:28) "to a depraved mind." God sends storms of chastisement on his people when they are out of his will. The wind and the rain that beat against us are God's way of getting us to wake up and come to our senses.

However, before we point a finger of accusation at Jonah, we must ask the question, "What about us?" Are we fulfilling our purpose? Are we in the will of God? Or have we too left his will and found a boat for Tarshish? One thing is certain, when we leave the Lord, we leave our aspirations behind also.

II. OBLIGATIONS

> Then the Lord sent a great wind on the sea, and such a violent storm arose that the ship threatened to break up. All the sailors were afraid and each cried out to his own god. And they threw the cargo into the sea to lighten the ship. But Jonah had gone below deck, where he lay down and fell into a deep sleep. The captain went to him and said, "How can you sleep? Get up and call on your god! Maybe he will take notice of us, and we will not perish" (Jonah 1:4-6).

The crew was frantic. They were praying to their own gods. Those rugged sailors had seen many a storm on the Mediterranean Sea. It would take quite a storm to get them alarmed.

And Jonah? He was indifferent and unconcerned. In fact, he was sound asleep. That shouldn't surprise us. This usually happens to men and women who leave God. They leave their obligations behind as well. Jonah was the only man on board the ship who knew God. He was the only man who could lay hold of God—and he was asleep. He had left his obligations.

While the others on board were fighting for their lives, Jonah was sleeping through the storm. He was really no different from a lot of professing Christians who are in the same boat today. So many of us seem to be at ease while the ship is sinking. So many people seem to be asleep while the storm is raging.

What is happening to this nation in which we are living? This ship we call America is in the midst of a storm and has been close to sinking while Christians have been in the bottom of the ship asleep. We have put a creed on our coins that says: "In God we trust." The Declaration of Independence says we are "endowed by our Creator with certain inalienable rights." The Mayflower Compact declares that America was established for the "glory of God and the advancement of the Christian faith." This very America is now in a storm. All of those affirmations of our heavenly Father are being stripped from before our eyes. We have come a long way as a nation since George Washington said in his farewell address on September 19, 1796, "Of all the dispositions and habits which lead to a political prosperity, religion and morality are indispensable supports. In vain would that man claim the tribute of patriotism, who should labor to subvert these great pillars of human happiness."

While we Christians have been sleeping in the ship, the Supreme Court banned prayer in public schools in 1963. Christmas carols have been prohibited in many schools. The courts have stripped the ten commandments from public school walls. Crosses in some city parks have been declared unconstitutional. Like Jonah, we are endangering the souls of others by being out of the will of God. Like Jonah, we had better wake up before it is too late.

The Bible says that the Lord sent the storm (Jonah 1:4). What should I do if my children disobey me? If I am really a loving parent, should I say, "Well, that's all right, honey"? Or should I discipline them? How do we know if we love our children? We discipline them. The Bible says, "The Lord disciplines those he loves, and he punishes everyone he accepts as a son" (Hebrews 12:6). Every once in a while some mother will say, "I just can't whip little Bobby because I love him so much!" But the Bible says that's not love. In fact, the Bible says, "He who spares the rod hates his son, but he who loves him is careful to discipline him" (Proverbs 13:24). If we really love our children we will discipline them.

God is too merciful and too loving to let his children drift into open rebellion without disciplining them. David said, "Before I was afflicted I went astray, but now I obey your word" (Psalm 119:67). "It was good for me to be afflicted so that I might learn your decrees" (Psalm 119:71). Why does God send the storms? In Jonah's case it was because he would no longer hear and obey. And some of us wonder why a storm is raging around us right now. It may be that it is the voice of a loving Father disciplining us, and in his mercy not giving us over to wrongdoing.

It is hard to believe that Jonah could sleep in such a storm. It shows how insensitive we can become. Sin hardens the heart. When we are on the run from the Lord's will, it is inevitable that we become spiritually insensitive.

Paul said in the Ephesian letter, "They are darkened in their understanding and separated from the life of God because of the ignorance that is in them due to the hardening of their hearts. Having lost all sensitivity, they have given themselves over to sensuality so as to indulge in every kind of impurity, with a continual lust for more" (Ephesians 4:18-19). (In the KJV verse 19 starts with the phrase, "who being past feeling.") Those words bear with them the picture of a callus. In fact, some translations use the adjective *callous* instead of "past feeling." A callus is skin that has lost its sensitivity. Most athletes know what it is to have calluses on the bottom of their feet. Seamstresses know what it is to have calluses on their fingers. You can stick a pin in a callus and not feel it; there is a loss of sensation.

This is what happens to our hearts if we continue in sin and leave the will of God. We become hard and without feeling toward God. We have no response to any spiritual stimulus. Do you remember the pain you felt the first time you committed some sin that really plagued your conscience? For children, perhaps it was a lie you told your parents. For others, it might have been an act of thievery, or an act of immorality. Think about it. Can you remember it? The hour of temptation came, you hesitated, you knew in your heart you shouldn't, but you finally said, "I'll try it just this once." And you fell. Do you remember the pain that came afterward? You went home. You couldn't bear the thought of facing those you love the most. You felt such shame. You were conscious that the eye of God had been upon you. You felt unclean. You were concerned about what others would think. You got into your bed and thought, "If that moment could only be lived over again, I'd never do it again." Oh, the pain you felt in your heart.

Then came the second time. The temptation came again. Again you succumbed. Afterward the pain was there, but it was a little less. And the third time, and the fourth, and on and on and on. Now you continue in that sin, and it scarcely bothers you. Your conscience is not affected by it anymore. You started on a walk of insensitivity. Your heart has become hardened.

The psalmist said, "Today, if you hear his voice, do not harden your hearts" (Psalm 95:7-8). Every time God calls us and we say no, continuing enroute to Tarshish, we become a little less sensitive. The callus on our hearts gets a little thicker. Before long we are totally insensitive to his call. Now that doesn't mean He has stopped calling; He continues to call. But the problem is, we can no longer hear. We are asleep. We are on a path of insensitivity that the apostle said is "past feeling." Those are haunting words.

I am writing to some whose hearts used to warm to the gospel. You used to aspire to the great things of God. You used to take seriously your obligation as a Christian. But something happened. You turned aside and tried to forget what God wanted of you.

If I were outside the will of God and felt no chastisement

from him, I would begin to examine myself to see if I was in the faith, or if God had given me over to a depraved or reprobate mind. Paul said that some folks go on in sin and "give themselves over." When a person makes a willful decision to leave God, after a certain point God will let that person go. In the greatest doctrinal treatise ever written, the book of Romans, Paul said:

> Therefore God gave them over in the sinful desires of their hearts to sexual impurity for the degrading of their bodies with one another. They exchanged the truth of God for a lie, and worshiped and served created things rather than the Creator—who is forever praised. Amen. Because of this, God gave them over to shameful lusts. Even their women exchanged natural relations for unnatural ones. In the same way the men also abandoned natural relations with women and were inflamed with lust for one another. Men committed indecent acts with other men, and received in themselves the due penalty for their perversion. Furthermore, since they did not think it worthwhile to retain the knowledge of God, he gave them over to a depraved mind, to do what ought not to be done" (Romans 1:24-28).

The Old Testament says it like this: "Ephraim is joined to idols; leave him alone!" (Hosea 4:17). Most persons who are out of the will of God are like Jonah in that they have not necessarily been given over, but they have been "overtaken in sin," as Paul talked about in the Galatian letter.

Jonah slept on while the storm raged. It is interesting that we really don't know when we are asleep. Recently, after returning home from Saturday church visitation, I sat in a chair in the den to rest for a while and in just a moment I looked at my watch and I had slept in that chair for an hour. I didn't know it. I thought, "Was I asleep?" So many people are not aware that they are asleep in the midst of the storm.

Further, when we are asleep, we dream of doing things we would never do when we are awake. Such was the case with Jonah. When we are sleeping through the storm, we don't like to hear the sound of an alarm. We want to sleep on. We are so comfortable. Most of us know that experience. It's the same spiritually. This is why messages and books that sound the alarm today rub many people the wrong way. They do not like to hear the alarm. They would rather go on in their sleep. They would rather listen to some positivist preacher who makes them feel comfortable in their sin.

The trouble with Jonah was that he was content with his rebellion. As long as our hearts are broken over our sin, as long as it keeps us awake at night, there is hope for us. But when we become comfortable in our sin, it is a danger signal. Many Christians are now content with uselessness. Some who used to cringe at the thought of certain social evils now are not bothered by those things. It is possible to be on the run from God's will even if we are not going anywhere.

Even though Jonah had forgotten God, God had not forgotten him. He continued in love to discipline and chase down his prophet. A little later we will see how far He went to get his attention.

Oh, that we would hear God's voice today. What do we mean, raising our children in "Christian homes" and not praying with them daily? What do we mean, saying we are Christians and our lives do not match our lips? What do we think we're doing—sleeping through the storm?

III. COMMUNICATIONS

> Then the sailors said to each other, "Come, let us cast lots to find out who is responsible for this calamity." They cast lots and the lot fell on Jonah (Jonah 1:7).

When we leave the will of God we leave the ability to hear God. Jonah had a God who spoke to him. When he left the will of God, he also left his ability to communicate with God.

Listen to the captain of the ship. When the waves of death were lashing against his ship, he suddenly believed in prayer. Fair-weather sailors are found not just in the open sea; they are found in the church of the Lord Jesus Christ. It is interesting in our part of the world that when the hurricanes come the television commentators who interview people hear lots of comments like, "We are boarding up and praying a lot." "We hope the good Lord spares us." "We are trusting in the Lord." It's strange that we hear people interviewed by these commentators the rest of the year and never hear anything like that until the storms come. It is the same with church members.

But Jonah? He was not praying. There is no evidence here that Jonah called on God. Later he did, but not here. Do you know why? He couldn't. He was regarding sin in his heart, and God would not hear him. So often our praying seems ineffective—and it is. The Bible says, "If I had cherished sin in my heart, the Lord would not have listened" (Psalm 66:18). Isaiah put it this way: "Surely the arm of the Lord is not too short to save, nor his ear too dull to hear. But your iniquities have separated you from your God; your sins have hidden his face from you, so that he will not hear" (Isaiah 59:1-2).

When we live with open and unrepented sin in our lives, we cannot communicate with God. There is a sense in which what we are when we pray is more important than what we pray.

The sailors cast lots. Does that mean it is all right to gamble? Is it all right to take part in a lottery? Although we see the casting of lots other times in the Old Testament, it is not right for us under the new covenant. Rather, we are to live by faith in our God.

The storm was raging, and the inevitable had to come. It always does. We can hide for a little while, but sooner or later we will be found out. Jonah learned this and so have many of us. The Bible says, "Be sure your sin will find you out" (Numbers 32:23).

It is a sad day when a saint of God has to be exposed before an unbelieving world, but that is what happened to Jonah. My heart is broken over verse 7. Every time one of us falls, it hurts the cause of the Lord Jesus Christ. Our hearts should grieve over what happened on this ship.

Since Jonah would not listen to God, God had to speak to him through the storm and through the sailors. Some of the storms of our lives occur because that is the only way God can get our attention.

IV. REPUTATIONS

> So they asked him, "Tell us, who is responsible for making all this trouble for us? What do you do? Where do you come from? What is your country? From what people are you?" He answered, "I am a Hebrew and I worship the Lord, the God of heaven, who made the sea and land." This terrified them and they asked, "What have you done?" (They knew he was running away from the Lord because he had already told them so.) (Jonah 1:8-10).

Jonah was the only man on board that ship who knew the living God and now, in leaving that God, he had also left his reputation.

A powerless Christian is pitiful to behold. "If the salt loses its saltiness . . . it is no longer good for anything" (Matthew 5:13). Some of us once gave the world a good taste of Jesus, but now as far as the kingdom is concerned, we are not "good for anything." Like Jonah, we hurt the testimony of Christ if we claim to be Christians and do not live like it.

Dr. R. T. Kendall tells a story of some youngsters who played a prank on a man with a moustache. They put limburger cheese on his moustache while he was taking a nap. When he awoke he said, "This bed stinks." He got up and walked around the room and said, "This room stinks." He went into another room, took a deep breath, and said, "This whole house stinks." He walked outside, took a deep breath, and said, "The whole world stinks!" Could it be that we are the ones who are making everyone else miserable by our rebellion against God? Oh, we are quick to blame them and feel that if they only started acting right, things would be wonderful.

This is the tragedy of backslidden Christians. They make everybody else miserable, and so it was with Jonah on the ship to Tarshish.

The thing that gets to me most about this part of Jonah's pilgrimage is that he had lost his testimony. It's amazing to note the questions with which Jonah was bombarded in these few verses. Think about it. "How can you sleep?" "Who is responsible?" "What do you do?" "Where do you come from?" "What is your country?" "From what people are you?" "What have you done?" "What should we do to you?" Could it be that people around us are asking the same questions?

It is a very sad day when a prophet of the Lord has to be asked, "What is your occupation?" "Who are you?" If someone has been around us for a period of time, and has to ask us if we are Christians, that is proof that we are outside the will of God.

And what about the question Jonah was asked, "Why have you done this?" (1:10 KJV)? What a rebuke. And this question came from a lost man. How humiliating.

But let me ask you, Why have you left the will of God? Listen to this question again: How could you have done this? Why did you do this? Because God is so cruel you didn't want to follow him? Is it that you just couldn't trust him? Was it that you didn't believe his word? Were you simply tired of him? Have you found a better friend? Was He unfaithful to his promise? Why? May the Holy Spirit press that question to our hearts.

We used to sing, "I've found a Friend, O such a Friend, He loved me ere I knew Him." We used to work with those dirty-faced little bus kids. We used to find our joy in seeing folks come to Christ. Why has all that come to an end? I'll tell you why. We found a ship. We got on board to flee from the will of God. But if any reader of this book is on the ship to Tarshish today, a loving God is chasing you down as he did Jonah. The Bible says, "Let the wicked forsake his way and the evil man his thoughts. Let him turn to the Lord, and he will have mercy on him, and to our God for he will freely pardon" (Isaiah 55:7).

The question is not "Why?" The question is "What?" What will we do about it? Will we go on in our rebellion or will we come back to Christ?

Jonah was found out. He had concealed his identity. Why do we point a finger of accusation at him? Some of us have worked in an office for years and not let anyone know we are Christians. How embarrassing it must have been for Jonah to admit this when his life was so different from his lips: "I worship the Lord." His practice had not matched his profession. Of this type person Jesus said, "These people honor me with their lips, but their hearts are far from me" (Matthew 15:8). Many persons profess to fear God today but their "saying and not doing" is nothing but blatant hypocrisy. Is it any wonder the church has lost so much influence?

Jonah's testimony didn't mean much, did it? This ought to be a lesson for all of us. Jonah was quick to say, "I worship God." But he didn't. If he did he would have been enroute to Nineveh.

Who fears God today? Have you really met anyone lately who fears the Lord? Men and women are not afraid of God today. So many of our churches seek to make sinners comfortable in their sin. They do not want to sound the alarm. This chapter is a call for us to awaken from our slumber. The alarm is sounding. We may want to reach over and turn it off, but we had better wake up before it is eternally too late.

Is there a Jonah reading these words? A Jonah who has fled from God's will? Know that you will be a very unhappy fugitive. God will not let you go unpunished if you are one of his. He will follow you. He will pursue you. He is the "hound of heaven." The storm will come.

Thank God for the storm. Have you thought about it? God did not have to send the storm. He could have let Jonah go on in his rebellion. He could have cut him off.[1] The storm was a sign that God was not finished with Jonah yet, and it just might be a sign that God is not finished with us yet. Remember, God sent the storm. Some of us have been blaming the storm experiences of life for our difficulties, when all the while it has been a loving Father calling us home. Let it remind us that we left our aspirations, obligations, communications, and reputations when we left the Lord. Jonah finally admitted, "I am a Hebrew." Who are you?

---

1. Kendall, R. T. 1978. *Jonah.* London: Hodder & Stoughton, p. 41.

CHAPTER THREE
Calming the Storm
Jonah 1:11-17

I. REASONS FOR THE STORM
II. REACTIONS TO THE STORM
III. RESULTS OF THE STORM

None of us is immune to the storms of life. The great hymns of our faith were written out of the crucible of experience. "It Is Well with My Soul" was written by H. G. Spafford immediately after he received news that his four daughters had been lost at sea.

The real issue is how we deal with the storms that come our way. Some of us simply fuss about them as the Israelites did when they asked God, "Why have you brought us out of Egypt? Are you just going to let us die in the wilderness?" Others of us respond to the storms of life as Job did. Job feared them. When Job lost his wealth, health, and family he said, "What I feared has come upon me" (Job 3:25). Still others of us are like Jonah. We flee. Jonah was on the run, but (as we have seen) he soon learned he could not flee forever.

Three factors enable us to deal with the storms of life in such a way that they can become calm. There are reasons for the storm. Before we can experience calm, we must discern what brought about the storm in the first place. There are reactions to the storm. Several ways in which people can react to the storms of life are illustrated by Jonah and those on board the ship. There is a sense in which the test of our Christian character is not in our actions but in our reactions. Finally, there are results of the storm. Once we have discerned the reasons for our storms and reacted properly, there comes an amazing result. The Bible says, "The raging sea grew calm."

I. REASONS FOR THE STORM

> The sea was getting rougher and rougher. So they asked him, "What should we do to you to make the sea calm down for us?" "Pick me up and throw me into the sea," he replied, "and it will become calm. I know that it is my fault that this great storm has come upon you" (Jonah 1:11-12).

"What shall we do with you?" That is quite a question, isn't it? In every storm of life it is important to get to the root, the cause, of it. In the midst of our storms, many of us are far more concerned with the cure than the cause. The reason we cannot find the cure is that we have not discovered the cause. It is strange that when the storms come, we never want to deal with the reasons for them. Instead, we are obsessed with the cure. In calming those storms, the place to begin is with the reasons for the storm.

Some of the storms of life are inevitable. There is a new wave of preaching that says if a storm of life comes, a sickness or a setback, it is because of one of two things: either we have sin in our lives or we do not have enough faith to overcome. But Jesus said that the Father "sends rain on the righteous and the unrighteous" (Matthew 5:45). Some things come our way because we are fallen men and women. This is a fallen world.

Other storms come our way for testing. This was certainly the reason for Job's storm. There is a difference between testing and trials. Testing comes from God to cause the Christian to stand. Trials come from Satan to cause the Christian to stumble. It is not unusual to find that many storms come our way to test our faith. Much of the epistle of James is written concerning this very point.

The reason for other storms of life is discipline. This was true of Jonah's case. A storm was raging as a result of his going his own way, rebelling against the will of God.

If the storm is a storm of testing, God is able to give victory through it. James said, "Consider it pure joy whenever you face trials." If your storm is a storm of chastisement or discipline, then punishment might be severe until you repent. Peter said:

> If you are insulted because of the name of Christ, you are blessed, for the Spirit of glory and of God rests on you. If you suffer, it should not be as a murderer or thief or any other kind of criminal, or even as a meddler. However, if you suffer as a Christian, do not be ashamed, but praise God that you bear that name (1 Peter 4:14-16).

One can hardly believe how stubborn human nature is until we see Jonah. At this stage of his flight, he would rather die than do the will of God. How stubborn we are sometimes. Like Jonah, some of us let pride so rule our lives that we would rather die than do God's will. Even reading these words, some persons may grit their teeth and stiffen their backs. We do not want to humble ourselves before the mighty hand of God.

The sea was getting rougher and rougher; the storm was intensifying. It was becoming virtually impossible to steer the ship, which was about to break in half.

Now remember, God had sent the storm. Some of us have the idea that God is like an old man with a long white beard looking feebly down on our experience on this planet and simply smiling and overlooking our sin. No, a thousand times no! To know how serious God is about our sin, we need to look at Calvary. God is so serious about sin that He gave his only Son to die for it. He is not looking down with a little smirk on his face, ignoring our sin. If we are his children and we are in open rebellion, He will pursue us and chase us down, and if we will not hear him, a storm of life will come about to get our attention.

Look at Jonah. His storm came to bring him to his senses.

But he still refused to take God's message to Nineveh.

An encouraging thing to me about this whole encounter is that God still used him after he had gone to Joppa, found a ship, left the will of God, and headed toward Tarshish. God still used him. A great revival eventually came to Nineveh. So often some of us think, "I've failed. God can never use me again." The storm, however, just might be there as an indication that God is not through with us yet. God did not have to send the storm. He could have let Jonah go on in his rebellion. He could have cut him off. He could let us go. But the reason for the storm often is that God still wants to use us.

The storm was there to teach Jonah a valuable lesson. God has a purpose in a continuing storm. If we are his children and we turn away from his will, we should not be surprised when storm clouds gather. "The Lord disciplines those he loves, and he punishes everyone he accepts as a son" (Hebrews 12:6). It is a good indication that we are his children when the storms come. "If you are not disciplined (and everyone undergoes discipline), then you are illegitimate children and not true sons" (Hebrews 12:8). When storms come, many Christians say, "God must be angry at me. I sinned and I knew that something like this would happen." Others are saying, "Twenty years ago I did this (or I did that) and this is just God's way of getting even." That is extremely faulty thinking. Listen to Psalm 103:3: "He does not treat us as our sins deserve or repay us according to our iniquities." If God dealt with us according to our sins, we would be chastised every moment of every day.

God does not get even by sending storms our way. God got even, so to speak, on the cross of Calvary. "We all, like sheep, have gone astray, each of us has turned to his own way; and the Lord has laid on him the iniquity of us all" (Isaiah 53:6). God's justice was satisfied at Calvary.

For Jonah the storm was the voice of God, as it was to Adam in his rebellion ("Where art thou?"), as it was to Elijah in his rebellion ("What are you doing here?").[1] What was the reason for Jonah's storm? A loving heavenly Father was getting the attention of his runaway prophet.

II. THE REACTIONS TO THE STORM

"Pick me up and throw me into the sea," he replied, "and
it will become calm. I know that it is my fault that this
great storm has come upon you." Instead, the men did
their best to row back to land. But they could not, for the
sea grew even wilder than before. Then they cried to the
Lord, "O Lord, please do not let us die for taking this
man's life. Do not hold us accountable for killing an innocent man, for you, O Lord, have done as you pleased"
(Jonah 1:12-14).

Once we discover the reason for our storm there are several
ways we might react. First, note the reaction of the sailors.
They rowed harder. They exerted themselves more and more
in strenuous activity. They did their best to row toward land.
Here was a group of men who tried in their own strength to
find a solution. "But they could not." Many people react like
that. They dig in deeper; they try harder; they work more dili-
gently. But they never make it.

The lesson here is that by our efforts alone we can never do
or be what God wants us to do or be. We can do our very best,
but our best is not good enough. In fact, the Bible says our
best is like "a filthy rag." Once in a while we hear someone say,
"Do your best for Jesus." It is a happy day in the life of believers when we realize that our best will not cut it. The secret is
allowing God to work his best through us, to let the Lord Jesus
Christ think through our minds, speak through our lips, walk
through our feet, touch through our hands, live through our
lives. So many Christians today attempt to live the Christian
life with the philosophy, "I'm going to try hard to be godly."
And so, with good intentions, they go out in their own power.
Andrew Murray once said, "The Christian life is not difficult;
it is impossible." We cannot live it. Our only hope in living the
Christian life is found in Colossians 1:27: "Christ in you, the
hope of glory." We must be filled, indwelt, and empowered by
the Holy Spirit.[2]

Frankly, I'm amazed at how many Christians live life like

these sailors; that is, by just trying harder. That may work for
Avis Rent-a-Car, but it is not the secret to victory in the Christian life. Some of this philosophy has come from a bestselling
Christian classic, the basic premise of which is that we should
walk in the steps of Jesus and do what Jesus did. When we get
to an intersection of life we stop and ask, "What would Jesus
do in this situation?" Then we simply do what He would do.
The problem with such an outlook is threefold.

First, it assumes that we always know what Jesus would do
in a certain situation. As I read the New Testament, I find He
was continually astounding the disciples because He was
always doing something new and saying something different.
Second, it assumes that once we know what Jesus would do,
we will go on and do it. If you are like me, and like Jonah, your
problem is not knowing what you ought to do but going on and
doing it. Third, the greatest fallacy of this philosophy is that
it presupposes that Jesus is not there. The question is, "If
Jesus were here, what would He do?" The marvelous truth is
that Jesus is here. If we are Christians, we are indwelt by him.
Christ is in us. It is not a matter of our trying to do what He
would do; the secret is in allowing him to do it in us and
through us.

As hard as they tried, the sailors could not get back to land.
We need to hear those words. We may row as hard as we can
in our own strength, but that is not enough. So many of us
have found this to be true. We thought we could overcome
that temptation and we did our very best, "But we could not."
When marriage problems came, we thought we could overcome them by doing our very best, "But we could not." Many
people today are trying their best to solve the problems of life,
while all the time the storm clouds grow darker, the thunder
rolls.

It is futile to fight against God. We must come to the end of
ourselves and learn not to trust in our strength but in the Lord.
Paul was getting at that when he said, "I have been crucified
with Christ, and I no longer live, but Christ lives in me. The life
I live in the body, I live by faith in the Son of God, who loved
me and gave himself for me" (Galatians 2:20).

Note that these sailors tried two things before they surrendered to God's will. First, "they threw the cargo into the sea
to lighten the ship" (Jonah 1:5). They thought that by getting
rid of their cargo, they could ride out the storm.[3] Many believers are still trying this today. They attempt to calm the storm
by getting rid of their cargo. They try to get rid of certain
things in their lives. Some stop hanging out after work at the
bars. Some try to stop swearing. Others seek to cease lying.
Others give up immorality. We give up this and give up that,
but still we have no peace.

Finally, the other thing the sailors tried to do was row harder
to get to land. There was, however, one way they could be
saved and that was that Jonah had to be sacrificed. Jonah
brought it up. "Use me as a substitute, a sacrifice." But they
rowed all the harder. They are not different from so many persons today who, after hearing about this substitute for sin in
the Lord Jesus Christ, go on trying to row their way to heaven.

How do we react to the storms of life? Are you a reader who
is rowing hard in your own strength? Give up. It will only get
worse. Let go and let God have his way. If it is a storm of discipline, stop trying to calm the storm by simply throwing your
cargo overboard and rowing harder. What we all need to do
is fling ourselves totally on the Lord Jesus Christ and, as the
songwriter said, "Let go and let God have his wonderful way."

There is another way to react to the storms of life. Note the
way Jonah reacted. "Pick me up and throw me into the sea,
and it will become calm. I know that it is my fault that this
great storm has come upon you." Jonah had stopped running.
He had admitted his sin. Now he was submitting to God. He
took responsibility. Some of us never get to this place. Had
some of us been Jonah, we would simply have continued to
blame everyone else for the storm, and it would have continued to beat on us.

The men responded by asking a question, "What should we
do to you?" Those on board that ship believed in the doctrine
of substitution. Some practice it even today.[4] Somewhere at
this very moment someone is wringing the neck of a scrawny
chicken, letting the blood spill over a grotesque mud idol,

because he or she believes in substitutionary atonement. It was the first lesson God taught Adam and Eve when they sinned. God took a substitute, an innocent animal, and after slaying that animal took its skin to cover their nakedness.

But we are too sophisticated to want to talk about the fall of man. We hear only about the ascent of man. The evolutionary process is in vogue. Our children in public schools are not taught that human beings are fallen creatures; they are taught that we are ascending, getting better all the time. Humanism is the modern god. Man is all sufficient and needs no substitutionary atonement, they tell us. The truth is that those heathen sailors were a lot better off than many modern educators. At least they knew the truth of substitution, which one day would send the Lord Jesus to the cross of Calvary to die for our sins.

Jonah reacted to the storm by stopping his flight and surrendering to God. He offered to be a sacrifice. We see the truth vividly here. Human efforts cannot calm the storms of God's judgment on sin. There must be a sacrifice. At this point Jonah became a picture, a foreshadow, of our Lord Jesus Christ.

How could Jonah make such a request? Was he suicidal? Was he self-destructive? No, he had finally begun to react properly. He realized that his life was not his own. Eight hundred years later our Lord would put it like this: "Whoever wants to save his life will lose it, but whoever loses his life for me and for the gospel will save it" (Mark 8:35).

We often are prone to forget this paradoxical principle of our Lord. We try to hold on, try to solve our own problems, by doing the work of the Holy Spirit ourselves. I believe that when Jonah said, "Throw me in," he was saying, "I'm flinging myself on the Lord and returning to his will."

None of us will ever get to this place until we sense God's love and concern for us individually. Like Jonah, when we sense that, we will let go of our lives. We will lose our lives so that we might really find them.

One test of Christian character is not our actions but our reactions. Jesus delivered the entire sermon on the mount to

teach us the importance of our reactions. He said, "If a man
slaps you on the cheek, turn the other also." He said, "If he
asks for your cloak, give him your coat also."

Jonah eventually reacted to the storm with submission to
God's will. We too must cease our flight from God's will and
surrender to him.

III. RESULTS OF THE STORM

Then they took Jonah and threw him overboard, and the
raging sea grew calm. At this the men greatly feared the
Lord, and they offered a sacrifice to the Lord and made
vows to him. But the Lord provided a great fish to swallow Jonah, and Jonah was inside the fish three days and
three nights (Jonah 1:15-17).

What a result! "The raging sea grew calm." When? It grew
calm when Jonah discovered that the reason for the storm was
his flight from God's will. And then he reacted properly by
ceasing his flight and surrendering to the Lord. Some storms
continue to rage because we never discern the cause, or
because we react with stubbornness.

When Jonah was in rebellion against the will of God, the sky
was dark, the thunder rolled, the lightning flashed, the winds
blew, the waves beat against the ship, and the rain fell in tor-
rents from the sky. The moment he surrendered to God's will
for his life, peace came. Calm. The clouds rolled away. The
waves fell down flat and gently thumped against the sides of
the ship. The sky became a beautiful blue. A gentle sea breeze
blew.

Peace came when Jonah began obeying the will of God.
More was accomplished in one moment in God's will than in
hours of tense toil and labor. How slow we are to grasp this
truth. The secret is in surrender.

God accepted the offering of Jonah. Our Lord Jesus said:

A wicked and adulterous generation asks for a miraculous
sign! But none will be given it except the sign of the

prophet Jonah. For as Jonah was three days and three nights in the belly of a huge fish, so the Son of Man will be three days and three nights in the heart of the earth. The men of Nineveh will stand up at the judgment with this generation and condemn it; for they repented at the preaching of Jonah, and now one greater than Jonah is here (Matthew 12:39-41).

Jonah was a sign of the Lord's death and resurrection. Our Lord showed us a picture of one greater than Jonah who one day would go to Calvary, into the grave, and rise again in order to offer himself as a sacrifice that others might be saved.

When the raging sea grew calm, the sailors feared the Lord, offered sacrifice, and made vows to God. They called on the name of the Lord. They had cried to "Yahweh" (Jonah 1:14). Previously, they had been "calling upon their gods" (Jonah 1:5). What a transformation had taken place in their lives.

The new-age philosophy running rampant across the world today tells us that we are all going to the same place, Buddhists and Hindus and Muslims alike. They have been teaching us songs like: "We are the world; we are the people." As believers in the Lord Jesus Christ, we are not the world. We are the church. We are in the world but not of the world. New-age thinking sounds like the philosophy of the sailors, where they "each cried out to his own god." It didn't matter to them which god they served. But note an interesting thing when deliverance came. They began calling on the name of the Lord. The same thing happened on mount Carmel when Elijah was facing the prophets of Baal. He challenged them to call on the name of their god and he would call on the name of the Lord and the deity that answered with fire would be the true and living God. "Everyone who calls on the name of the Lord will be saved" (Romans 10:13). "Salvation is found in no one else, for there is no other name under heaven given to men by which we must be saved" (Acts 4:12).

Those sailors made promises to God. They said, "We are going to do some things differently." They made their promises after the sea became calm. A lot of us promise God all sorts of things when the storm is raging and then we forget them when the storm passes by. These men made their promises, and thanksgiving after the storm. How many of us have been in the midst of a storm and promised God something we never kept when the sea was calm? It was only when these rough sailors were willing to admit they could not by their own efforts save themselves, when they flung themselves on God's remedy, that they were truly saved.

They were not saved because they offered sacrifices; they offered the sacrifices because they were saved. Works are not for salvation. These men offered their sacrifices after the sea had calmed. Good works are the fruit of salvation. The Bible says, "We are God's workmanship, created in Christ Jesus to do good works, which God prepared in advance for us to do" (Ephesians 2:10). They said to God, "You have done as you pleased." Here is proof that these men were transformed. They surrendered to the sovereignty of the Lord God. God is sovereign, which simply means He does what He pleases (and He is always pleased with what He does). This is one reason more folks do not come to Christ: they do not want to bend to his sovereignty. They would rather do as they please than allow God to do as He pleases in their lives.

These callous-handed sailors saw the need for atonement. They also saw that it was outside themselves. No one will ever be saved as long as he thinks he can do it in his own strength. We need a substitute, and one has been provided for us in the Lord Jesus Christ.

What was the result of the storm? For the sailors, they greatly feared the Lord and offered a sacrifice to him as they made vows to him. When we see the reason for our storms and react properly to them, we will see similar results. The raging sea will grow calm. We will acknowledge that the Lord can do as He pleases in our lives, and we will make our lives a living sacrifice to his glory.

What was the result of the storm in the life of Jonah? God saved him, and used a fish to prepare him for revival. Jonah had resigned himself to death. But God appointed a great fish to preserve his runaway prophet. God did not want to kill Jonah; He wanted to save him. It's the same with us. The belly of a great fish is not a happy place to live. But for those in rebellion, it is a healthy place to learn. Had it not been for the fish's belly, many of us would not be living for Christ in victory today. We do not learn spiritual lessons on the mountaintop. We learn them down in the valley.

I am always a little amused at the way Christians think they need to prove the possibility of a miracle. While I was preaching for several months through the book of Jonah in our church, several well-meaning people gave me articles explaining how it is possible for a person to live a certain number of days in the belly of a large fish—because the stomach gases emit enough oxygen, and other explanations of the miraculous. I have read documented accounts of men who survived for days inside a fish. Why is it that we always think we have to explain the miraculous? What happened to Jonah was a miracle. Take away the miraculous from Jonah and you destroy the miraculous of the gospel—the death, burial, and resurrection of our Lord.

This great fish is an object lesson about the mercy of God. God performed a miracle to preserve his man. God specializes in doing that. He'll do the same for us when we surrender to him. Shortly after my conversion I remember singing a little chorus at youth camp. It went like this:

Are there any rivers that seem to be uncrossable?
Are there any mountains you cannot tunnel through?
God specializes in things that seem impossible;
He knows a thousand ways to make a way for you.

Although we may forsake God, He never forsakes us (Deuteronomy 31:6; Hebrews 13:5). God has promised never to leave us nor forsake us. Many of us can remember a time when we turned and went our own ways, but not one of us can recall a time when God has turned on us. There is no shadow of turning in God. He is faithful. Great is his faithfulness.

Do you see what is happening in the pilgrimage of our

prophet? Jonah was saving his life by losing it. Previously God had commanded him to go to Nineveh and Jonah said no. He grabbed tighter to his life. God said *go*, and Jonah said *no*. He clutched his life all the tighter and in possessing his life, he lost it. He lost joy, freedom, happiness, purpose. He lost his high calling and he found himself in the midst of a storm. He is not different from many of us. So many people today are clutching their own lives, not willing to let go and let God have his way. The tragedy is that in holding their lives so tightly they are losing them. "For whoever wants to save his life will lose it, but whoever loses his life for me and for the gospel will save it" (Mark 8:35).

Do you see it? Jonah let go of his life. He said, "Throw me overboard." And when he let go of his life, he found it. A lot of Christians are in trouble today because they will not let God have their lives. When the storm comes, we grit our teeth, throw out a little cargo, row a little harder, and the harder we work in clutching our lives, the worse the storm becomes and the more of our joy and purpose and peace we lose. Some of us are concentrating too much on the second part of Jesus' commandment; that is, on "finding our life." We ought to be concentrating on the first part, "losing our life." This is the fallacy of a lot of modern psychology. We hear from many circles that we must "find ourselves." The way really to find ourselves is to lose ourselves in the love of the Lord Jesus Christ. To lose our lives in Christ means to take our hands off it, to surrender totally to him and say, "Lord, here's my life; take it and use it to your glory."

The Old Testament is full of shadows (or types) of Christ. You have never seen a sunrise until you see it rise over the Atlantic Ocean on Fort Lauderdale beach. You can stand on our beach and your shadow will stretch across the beach and across the street to the building beyond. No one could ever make out the fact that it was a human shadow. But a strange thing happens as the sun continues to rise. If you were to keep standing on the beach, by ten a.m. your shadow would be in complete proportion to your body and would be easily identifiable. By high noon there would be no shadow at all.

The Sun of God's revelation began to shine in those early chapters of Genesis. It rose there with the slaying of the innocent animal to cover Adam and Eve's sin. It rose a little higher with Abel's offering, and still higher with Abraham and Isaac. Then came the Passover lamb, and the shadow was coming more into focus. Jonah in the fish's belly gives us a beautiful picture. We come to Isaiah 53 with the suffering servant. There we see a perfect shadow, a perfect picture of our Lord Jesus Christ. Finally came the day when high noon on God's clock of revelation struck, when God became flesh and dwelt among us in the body of our Lord Jesus. But one of the clearest pictures of the coming Christ in the Old Testament is found here in Jonah.

The storm beat on Jonah in the ship because of sin, and sin must be punished by death. The guilty must die. The Bible says, "The soul that sins, it shall surely die." "The wages of sin is death." What a picture we see in Jonah of Jesus who took the sinners' place. The Bible says, "God made him who had no sin to be sin for us, so that in him we might become the righteousness of God" (2 Corinthians 5:21). "We all, like sheep, have gone astray, each of us has turned to his own way; and the Lord has laid on him the iniquity of us all" (Isaiah 53:6). "He himself bore our sins in his body on the tree, so that we might die to sins and live for righteousness; by his wounds you have been healed" (1 Peter 2:24).

Here is the doctrine of substitutionary atonement; that is, one must die that others might live. Caiaphas, the high priest, must have surprised himself at the trial of Jesus by saying, "You know nothing at all! You do not realize that it is better for you that one man die for the people than that the whole nation perish. He did not say this on his own, but as high priest that year he prophesied that Jesus would die for the Jewish nation" (John 11:49-51).

Our Lord was cast into the sea of God's judgment to die and rise again for our redemption. This great ship of humanity was battered by the waves of judgment and was headed for destruction. There was only one way that such a storm could be stilled. "Jesus paid it all / All to him I owe / Sin had left a crimson stain / He washed it white as snow." Jonah was thrown overboard. Our Lord Jesus was nailed to the cross. "He was pierced for our transgressions, he was crushed for our iniquities; the punishment that brought us peace was upon him, and by his wounds we are healed" (Isaiah 53:5).

> Alas! and did my Savior bleed
> And did my sovereign die?
> Would He devote that sacred Head
> For sinners such as I?
>
> Was it for sins that I have done
> He suffered on the tree?
> Amazing pity! grace unknown!
> And love beyond degree!
>
> But drops of grief can ne'er repay
> The debt of love I owe;
> Here, Lord, I give myself away—
> 'Tis all that I can do!
>
> At the cross, at the cross,
> Where I first saw the light,
> And the burden of my heart rolled away—
> It was there by faith
> I received my sight,
> And now I am happy all the day.

Have you seen this savior as your personal substitute? There is only one way we can be saved, and that is to surrender to God and accept the gift of his Son, our substitute, who took our place on Calvary's mountain and died our death so that we might live his life.

Perhaps some of my readers find themselves in the belly of a fish this very moment saying, "How can I hold on?" How many people feel as if they have been swallowed by some great fish of life? It's dark, and confusion sets in. I'm sure Jonah felt that there was no way out of his dilemma.

It is wonderful to remember that Christ is at the right hand of the Father making intercession for us. I wonder what He would pray for those who find themselves in a fish belly today. I think He might be praying what He prayed for Peter: "I have prayed for you, Simon, that your faith may not fail. And when you have turned back, strengthen your brothers" (Luke 22:32).[5]

What a thought. Jesus prays for us at the right hand of the Father that "our faith may not fail." In the end, it is really our faith that matters. That is why Paul would say later, "I live by faith in the Son of God" (Galatians 2:20). If you are swallowed by doubt today, remember that there is one who is forever faithful in offering his prayers in perfect faith for you that your faith will not fail. Lose your life in him, and you will find it.

The raging sea grew calm. Those who were lost were saved. Those out of the will of God were recovered. Oh, that the result of our storms today might be that we see Jesus in Jonah, that we might see Jesus as our substitute.

> In the dark of the midnight
> Have I oft hid my face,
> While the storms howl above me
> And there's no hiding place,
> 'Mid the crash of the thunder,
> Precious Lord, hear my cry,
> Keep me safe 'til the storm passes by.
>
> Many times Satan whispered,
> "There is no use to try,
> For there's no end of sorrow,
> There's no hope by and by,"
> But I know Thou art with me,
> And tomorrow I'll rise
> Where the storms never darken the skies.
>
> When the long night has ended
> And the storms come no more,
> Let me stand in Thy presence
> On that bright, peaceful shore

In the land where the tempest
Never comes, Lord, may I
Dwell with Thee when the storm passes by.

'Til the storm passes over,
'Til the thunder sounds no more,
'Til the clouds roll forever from the sky,
Hold me fast, let me stand
In the hollow of Thy hand,
Keep me safe 'til the storm passes by.

---

1. Martin, Hugh. 1890. *Jonah.* Carlisle PA: Banner of Truth Trust, p. 178.
2. Draper, James T., Jr. 1971. *Jonah: Living in Rebellion.* Wheaton IL: Tyndale House Publishers, p. 42.
3. Dehaan, M. R. 1957. *Jonah: Fact or Fiction.* Grand Rapids MI: Zondervan Publishing House, p. 50.
4. Smith, James and Robert Lee. 1947. *Handfuls on Purpose.* Grand Rapids MI: Wm. B. Eerdmans Publishing Co., Vol. X, p. 42.
5. Kendall, R. T. 1978. *Jonah.* London: Hodder & Stoughton, p. 96.

CHAPTER FOUR
You Can't Keep
A Good Man Down
Jonah 2:1-10

The pages of history are filled with the heartwarming stories of men and women who have been down and have come back. In the field of politics we immediately think of Abraham Lincoln. No one has ever descended deeper into a fish's belly politically than did Lincoln. He was defeated for the state legislature in Illinois in 1832. He was defeated for Congress in 1843. He was defeated for Congress again in 1848. In 1855 he ran for the Senate and was defeated. He was on the vice presidential ticket in 1856 and was defeated again. He ran for the Senate in 1858 and was once more defeated. He became president in 1860 and lives on in history as one of the greatest presidents of the United States. Abraham Lincoln is proof that you can't keep a good man down.

In the field of literature I think of John Bunyan. He was thrown into prison where it would have been easy to give up and say, "What's the use?" But down in that dungeon he penned the words of *Pilgrim's Progress*, which have blessed millions through the generations. The truth is, you cannot keep a good man down.

We have seen it in our own generation with a man like Chuck Colson. He was humiliated before the world during the Watergate scandal. He too was placed in prison, but God used those experiences to make him one of the most effective proponents of the Christian faith in the world today. You cannot keep a good man down.

A similar mystique surrounds the success of some motion pictures. Something in all of us seems to rally around those who are down and out and who come back. Take the *Rocky* movies. Everybody loves to cheer for the poor street kid who was a loser and who comes back in glory. We love to see someone who, when it appears there is no way out, comes through.

Jonah lives on in history and in heaven to show us the truth that you cannot keep a good man down. Having been thrown overboard during the storm, he was swallowed by a great fish. For three days and nights he tossed in the belly of that monster as it journeyed into the depths of the sea, but finally the Bible records, "The Lord commanded the fish, and it vomited Jonah onto dry land." He wiped the seaweed off his face, and then the Bible says, "The word of the Lord came to Jonah a second time."

So many of us are in need of an escape today. So many women and men are longing to be out of the fish's belly of life where they feel so trapped. We often remain there until we learn some valuable lessons. It took Jonah three days and three nights to learn those lessons. How long will it take us to learn the lessons of getting out of the fish's belly? And what are those lessons?

I. A Man of Prayer

From inside the fish Jonah prayed to the Lord his God. He said: "In my distress I called to the Lord, and he answered me. From the depths of the grave I called for help, and you listened to my cry. You hurled me into the deep, into the very heart of the seas, and the currents swirled about me; all your waves and breakers swept over me. I said, 'I have been banished from your sight; yet I will look again toward your holy temple.' The engulfing waters threatened me, the deep surrounded me; seaweed was wrapped around my head. To the roots of the mountains I sank down; the earth beneath barred me in forever. But you brought my life up from the pit, O Lord my God" (Jonah 2:1-6).

There are some important questions for any inquirer to ask at this particular point in Jonah's pilgrimage. When did he pray? To whom did he pray? What did he pray? How did he pray? First, we note when he prayed.

At our church in Fort Lauderdale we have a new prayer chapel. It is beautifully furnished, luxuriously carpeted, and air-conditioned. It is a spot where any of our people can come to meet God in intercessory prayer. Jonah's prayer chapel was different. It was smelly, damp, dark, and dingy. It was the belly of a fish in constant motion. Jonah was in distress and he called out to the Lord from his prayer chapel. Some people do not pray in our prayer chapel. It is amazing that some of us wait until we are in a fish's belly, in distress, to call out to the Lord. But aren't we thankful to God we can pray then? Such was the case with Jonah. "He prayed in his distress."

In my days of pastoring churches, I have known a lot of Jonahs who have cried out to God in their distress and God heard them and delivered them. As a pastor I know what it is to see a father who never had time for his son. He was always too busy, working fourteen hours a day to be super-successful. His weekends were taken up with his friends at ballgames or on the fishing boat. The boy grew older and one day stood on a ball diamond at the Little League park patting his glove as he looked in the stands. But dad was not there. He was too busy for that. In fact, he was so busy trying to make a living he forgot to make a life. I have seen fathers like that who now sit and weep. "If only I had it all to do over again." His son is in trouble and is ruining his life. The father finds himself in a fish's belly. But listen: "In my distress I called on the Lord, and he answered me." Just because we may be in distress, we should not let our pride keep us from calling on the Lord.

As a pastor I know what it is to see a woman who has fallen victim to the flirtatious lies of her boss. She found a ship of seduction and sailed to Tarshish. She left a loving husband and precious children to follow the lust of the flesh, only to find that now her lover has left her for a younger woman, and all is gone. Gone is her self-worth. Gone is her self-respect. She finds herself in the fish's belly of shame and humiliation. But listen: "In my distress I called to the Lord, and he answered me." No matter who we are or where we are, we can call on God in our distress.

As a pastor I know what it is to see a young girl with tear-stained cheeks. Her goals had been so high. Her future had been so bright. She had a Christian boyfriend, but they could not wait. To some teenagers four years of college seems a long long time. They planned on being married some day. It seemed all right. And there she is, half girl and half adult, with big tears rolling out of big blue eyes. And the boy? He's gone now and doesn't want to see her any more. He is off to college and other more important things. There she sits with her faithful parents. "What will I do? My life is ruined." But listen: "In my distress I called to the Lord, and he answered me." The blood of Jesus Christ, God's Son, still cleanses us from all sin, and when He does cleanse us, we should never call unclean what He has cleansed.

We can always call out for help. Jonah's experience is a proclamation of hope. Jonah cried out in his distress and found deliverance—and so can we. The first step in getting out of the fish's belly is to call out to God, to pray. Some have tried everything: pills, books, counselors. But listen: "In my distress I called to the Lord, and he answered me."

The problem with many of us is that we are too proud to pray in our distress. We think we are doing God a favor by saying, "I didn't call on him before, so I don't want to trouble him now." Those who say that do not know the heart of this loving God. If you are in distress, it is all the more reason to call on the name of the Lord.

How low some of us come before we surrender to his will.

What sorrow and calamity some of us bring on ourselves through disobedience. Jonah prayed from the fish's belly. It is never too late to pray. It is never too late to get God into our circumstances.

Jonah had little hope of ever getting out of the fish's belly. But in his distress, he did what he could do, and that was to pray.

I often wonder what it is going to take to get some of us to pray. Could I be writing to a Jonah today? Could I be writing to some individuals who know God's will for their lives and are waiting until affliction comes their way to call them to repentance? The lesson here is that if we continue to go our own way in rebellion against God's will, the result is nothing but despair. Are you in a fish's belly? Then call on the Lord! No situation is too difficult for prayer. You cannot keep a good man down. Why? Because he is a man of prayer. And when does he pray? In his distress.

A second important aspect of Jonah's prayer is found in to whom he prayed. Even though he rebelled, he was in covenant relationship with God. He had a personal God. It was *his* God to whom he prayed. I am thankful that on January 3, 1965, as a seventeen-year-old in Fort Worth, Texas, I entered into covenant relationship with my God through the Lord Jesus Christ. I did not earn that relationship nor deserve it. I simply accepted the free gift of eternal life, and the Lord Jesus Christ came to live in my life. Today He is *my* God.

Do you see it? It is impossible to come to God and say, "Our Father," if we have never been born into his family. John 1:12 says, "Yet to all who received him, to those who believed in his name, he gave the right to become the children of God." In the Galatian epistle Paul said, "We are children of God by faith in Christ Jesus." It is true that we are all God's creation, but only those who trust in Christ are his children. Jonah could pray to *his* God. Can you?

Jonah had gone a long way from God but he never got away from the fact that God was his portion, his possession. Even though Jonah forsook the Lord, the Lord never forsook Jonah. He was still his God.[1]

When we pray to our God, we can come clean in confession.

So many people want to keep on their masks and never open up. Some are obsessed with wanting to be liked and accepted by their peers; they are afraid that if their peers really knew them, they would not like them or accept them. Consequently, there are a lot of people, especially young people, who project on others an image they want them to see so they will like them. For example, some teenagers wear designer jeans thinking that those jeans will cause other people to like them. Many young adults drive automobiles they cannot afford, hoping others will accept them. Happy is the man or woman who has been freed from that bondage.

It is one thing to behave in such a manner with others, but the tragedy comes when we attempt to do the same thing with God. Some pray as if they are trying to impress him. We need to remember that He knows us. Jonah prayed and was open and honest. It is a fallacy to think we can impress God by trying to act as if we are all right.

Some think that because they are saved they should never have any distress or affliction. My friend, Dr. Curtis Benton, a serious theologian and a successful eye surgeon, would be the first to tell you that if you have cataracts before your conversion, you will probably have them after your conversion. If you have gallstones before you come to Christ, chances are you will have them after you invite Christ into your heart. Some think that regeneration immediately solves all of our problems, especially emotional distress. Like the physical, often our emotional traumas are still there. God can and will deliver and set us free, but like Jonah we must be open with him.

Some believers today have broken fellowship with God and think they have broken relationship. However, as disobedient as Jonah was in his rebellion, as much as he had gone in the opposite direction of God's will for his life, he still realized that God was his God. Some of us have gone our own way, leaving the will of God, and have been battered by the storm and swallowed up into the fish's belly. Listen, there is good news. If we are really God's children, He is still our Father. Jonah prayed to the Lord his God, and so can we.

It is also important to note what Jonah prayed. In studying

his prayer we make a remarkable discovery. Jonah did not use one original thought or request in this petition. What did he do? Jonah simply prayed the word of God. He prayed the scriptures. Eight times in these few verses he quoted from the book of Psalms. Jonah said, "In my distress I called to the Lord, and he answered me. From the depths of the grave I called for help, and you listened to my cry" (Jonah 2:2). Where did he get that? Listen carefully to Psalm 18:6: "In my distress I called to the Lord; I cried to my God for help. From his temple he heard my voice; my cry came before him, into his ears." Listen to Psalm 120:1: "I call on the Lord in my distress, and he answers me." And Psalm 86:13: "For great is your love toward me; you have delivered my soul from the depths of the grave."

Jonah knew the word of God. Do you see what is happening in this prayer? Jonah is standing on the promises of God and praying the scriptures.

Jonah went on in his prayer to say, "You hurled me into the deep, into the very heart of the seas, and the currents swirled about me; all your waves and breakers swept over me" (Jonah 2:3). Now where did he get that? Listen to Psalm 88:6: "You have put me in the lowest pit, in the darkest depths." Psalm 42:7: "Deep calls to deep in the roar of your waterfalls; all your waves and breakers have swept over me." Do you see it? Jonah knew the word of God and was simply praying scriptures. He was reminding God of the many promises of prayer.

Jonah kept praying. "I said, 'I have been banished from your sight; yet I will look again toward your holy temple'" (Jonah 2:4). Where did he get that? Listen to Psalm 31:22: "In my alarm I said, 'I am cut off from your sight!' Yet you heard my cry for mercy when I called to you for help."

Jonah knew the Old Testament promises. He remembered them and he stood on them. He knew the promise of 2 Chronicles 6:36-39:

> When they sin against you—for there is no one who does not sin—and you become angry with them and give them over to the enemy, who takes them captive to a land far away or near; and if they have a change of heart in the

land where they are held captive, and repent and plead
with you in the land of their captivity and say, 'We have
sinned, we have done wrong and acted wickedly'; and if
they turn back to you with all their heart and soul in the
land of their captivity where they were taken, and pray
toward the land you gave their fathers, toward the city
you have chosen and toward the temple I have built for
your Name; then from heaven, your dwelling place, hear
their prayer and their pleas, and uphold their cause. And
forgive your people who have sinned against you.

Therefore, knowing these promises, Jonah said, "I have been
banished from your sight yet I will look again toward your holy
temple" (Jonah 2:4).

Jonah continued his prayer by saying, "The engulfing waters
threatened me, the deep surrounded me; seaweed was
wrapped around my head" (Jonah 2:5). Again he was quoting
the psalmist, who said in Psalm 69:1-2:

Save me, O God,
for the waters have come up to my neck.
I sink in the miry depths,
where there is no foothold.
I have come into the deep waters;
the floods engulf me.

Jonah concluded his prayer by saying, "To the roots of the
mountains I sank down; the earth beneath barred me in
forever. But you brought my life up from the pit, O Lord my
God" (Jonah 2:6). Where did Jonah get that? He got it from
Psalm 30:3, which says, "O Lord, you brought me up from the
grave; you spared me from going down into the pit."

Jonah had hid the word in his heart and, remembering it, he
stood on it by faith and prayed the scriptures. This is a marvelous way to make petitions to our God.

Parents should be praying scriptures over their children.
For example, we should be praying that "God might give them

the spirit of wisdom and revelation in the knowledge of Christ."
We should be praying scriptures for our friends that "God
might grant unto them to be strengthened with might by his
Spirit in the inner man." We should be praying the scriptures
over our missionaries, that "he who dwells in the shelter of the
Most High will rest in the shadow of the Almighty." It is no
wonder so many people stay in the fish's belly. They never call
out to the Lord their God in prayer.

Praying the scriptures does not begin with us. It begins in
the heart of God. We receive God's promise from above
through his word, quickened by the Holy Spirit, and that is
where we stand. Jonah began appealing to God on the basis
of his personal promises.

Jesus said, "If you remain in me and my words remain in
you, ask whatever you wish and it will be given you" (John
15:7). Are you abiding in the Lord Jesus? Is his word abiding
in you? If so, you will never ask him for anything that is con-
trary to his will. Therefore, He can promise you, "Ask what
you will, and it will be done unto you." Without the Bible,
prayer has no direction; and without prayer, the Bible has no
dynamic. God speaks to us through his written word, and we
speak to him through prayer. Can you see this taking place in
Jonah's prayer? Jonah's prayers were answered. Why are
some of our prayers unanswered? Could it be that too few of
us have been alone with God long enough to get a word from
him on which to stand? The Bible says, "Faith comes from
hearing the message, and the message is heard through the
word of Christ" (Romans 10:17).[2]

So many persons say they cannot pray more than two or
three minutes because they do not know what to pray. We
need to pray the word of God. If we are lost, the Bible says,
"Those who call on the name of the Lord shall be saved." So
we come to God and say, "Lord, you have said that whoever
calls on your name will be saved, so save me for Christ's sake."
Are you burdened? Then come to the Lord with his promise
and say, "Lord, you have said that you have borne my griefs
and carried my sorrows, so I put on the garment of praise for
the spirit of heaviness."

Are you lonely? Then come to the Lord on the basis of his word and say, "Lord, you have said you will never leave me nor forsake me. You have said, 'Do not fear, for I am with you: do not be dismayed, for I am your God. I will strengthen you and help you; I will uphold you with my righteous right hand'" (Isaiah 41:10).

Are you afraid? Come to God on the basis of his word and say, "Lord, you have said in what time I am afraid I can call upon you."

Are you in need? Then come to God on the basis of his word and say, "Lord, you have said you would meet all my needs according to your glorious riches in Christ Jesus."

Do you need forgiveness? Then come to the Lord and say, "Lord, you have said that if I confess my sin you would be faithful and just to forgive me and cleanse me of all unrighteousness. So I claim that promise and accept your forgiveness."

Blessing comes through obedience. Jonah had the word in his heart all along but he was not willing to heed it. You can have the word of the Lord in your heart and not heed it. Blessing comes in obedience to God's will. As soon as Jonah got back into God's will, he was released, set free from the bonds that had enslaved him. You cannot keep a good man down. Why? Because he is a man of prayer. When does he pray? In his distress. To whom does he pray? He prays to the Lord his God. What does he pray? He prays the word of God.

It is also important to observe how Jonah prayed. Jonah was down, depressed, in distress. But look what happened when he started praying the scriptures. "You brought my life up from the pit, O Lord my God." Where did he get the faith to pray that kind of prayer? He remembered Psalm 30:3. "O Lord, you brought me up from the grave, you spared me from going down into the pit." God quickened this verse in his heart and he stood on it by faith.

I am encouraged when I read these verses. Jonah's attitude of faith shows us that from God's perspective there is no such thing as a hopeless case. No matter how far one may have gone down, he or she can still call on the Lord in faith and be delivered.

II. A Man of Purpose

"When my life was ebbing away, I remembered you, Lord,
and my prayer rose to you, to your holy temple. Those
who cling to worthless idols forfeit the grace that could
be theirs" (Jonah 2:7-8).

Jonah came to realize that there had been a purpose in his pilgrimage. Paul said it like this: "And we know that in all things
God works for the good of those who love him, who have been
called according to his purpose" (Romans 8:28).

Dr. R. T. Kendall in his book *Jonah* made an astute observa-
tion here. He pointed out that Romans 8:28 means that just
because something has been made right does not mean it was
right.[3] Although it is true that God can make "all things work
together for good," this does not justify disobedience. As we
have noted, Jonah's chastening foreshadowed our Lord's
death, burial, and resurrection. But nonetheless we should not
try to justify Jonah's rebellion. There are people who try to
justify their sins simply because things turned out all right.
The fact that Jesus used Jonah's experience with the fish as a
picture of his own death, burial, and resurrection does not
mean that Jonah's rebellion was justified.

Some of us have become accomplished at trying to justify
our sin. As an example, we are reminded of David. He had
committed adultery with Bathsheba and had Uriah her husband murdered to cover his sin. For some it seems amazing
that in the genealogy of Jesus in Matthew 1 we read, ". . . And
Jesse the father of King David. David was the father of
Solomon, whose mother had been Uriah's wife." One might
say it worked out for good, so that made it right. No! Thank
God it can be made right, but that does not mean it was right.
Lest we forget, remember that David reaped what he sowed.
His heart was broken when his son Absalom rebelled against
him and lost his life. His daughter was abused—and on and
on we could go.

Jonah said, "I remembered the Lord." He was saying, "I
came to myself. The truth dawned on me." Then he con-

fessed, "I forgot God and listened to the lies of the devil. I've been clinging to the worthless idols of self, and have forfeited the grace that could have been mine all the while." It is interesting that Jonah said this when he got to the end of his rope. The way he termed it was "when my life was ebbing away." It seemed that things could get no worse. That phrase is literally translated "when I had lost all hope." Jonah had come to absolute helplessness.

Some of us simply have to get to the place where we have nowhere else to turn but to God, to the place where we have lost all hope unless He comes through.

I thank God He is always there. But how much easier it would have been on Jonah if he had remembered the Lord when he stepped up to the ticket booth at Joppa to buy his ticket to sail for Tarshish. To those of us who think we have found a ship to Tarshish and are about to purchase our ticket, "Remember the Lord!" Jonah put it this way, "Those who cling to worthless idols forfeit the grace that could be theirs."

The Lord allowed this stress to come into Jonah's life so that he might come to himself and remember the Lord. It was the same with the prodigal son. His father knew better. His father knew what was best for him, but out of love he let him go. Now, like the prodigal boy, the prodigal Jonah is coming home. He too has found out that clinging to worthless idols was not worth it.

In Jonah's dark and damp dungeon there did not seem to be a ray of hope, but suddenly the light of God's glory started coming in. What do you suppose he remembered? I think he remembered God's mercy. I think he must have remembered Lamentations 3:32: "Though he brings grief, he will show compassion, so great is his unfailing love."

Jonah knew well the emptiness of those idols. He had watched the sailors pray to their idols to no avail. Did he now realize that he was worshiping one of the worst of all idols: self?

Jesus died on the cross not only to set us free from sin, but also from self. The Bible says, "And he died for all, that those who live should no longer live for themselves but for him who died for them and was raised again" (2 Corinthians 5:15). Victory over self is claimed in the same way as victory over sin. We do not have victory over sin by trying to earn or deserve it. We are saved by faith. Victory over self is achieved in the same way: by faith.

Paul urged us not to be conformed any longer to the pattern of this world, but to be transformed by the renewing of our minds (Romans 12:2). A lot of us are trying to put away the idols of self by conforming, or by nonconforming. Nonconforming never produces victory. It is good that believers do not drink or smoke dope or wear suggestive clothing or go to x-rated movies or gamble or be involved in illicit sex or talk in a filthy manner. But where is the victory? It is not in conformity or in nonconformity. The victory comes from God. The victory is transformation within by faith. It is good that we throw our cargo overboard, but it will not bring our victory. We don't get victory; we *have* victory if we are truly converted. The problem is that some of us are not appropriating it. While some of us are so busy trying to get it, we forget we already have it—in Christ.

Jonah looked back, remembered the Lord, and the first thing out of his mouth was, "It wasn't worth it!" It is no sign of God's mercy if you are getting away with your sin. If you keep clinging to worthless idols, you keep forfeiting the grace that could be yours.

III. A Man of Praise

"But I, with a song of thanksgiving, will sacrifice to you. What I have vowed I will make good. Salvation comes from the Lord" (Jonah 2:9).

"Give thanks in all circumstances, for this is God's will for you in Christ Jesus" (1 Thessalonians 5:18). If Jonah could offer a sacrifice of praise from the belly of a fish, surely we can offer one from our distress.

Note that Jonah did not ask to be delivered. He simply started praising God in a difficult situation and giving thanks. All that most of us know about giving thanks is associated with good times. We give thanks at family times—for the turkey, the harvest, the business, the baby. Jonah learned something liberating. He learned that giving thanks in everything would set him free.

When midnight comes, when we find ourselves in distress, many of us feel like giving up and wallowing in self-pity. We lapse into a martyr complex. But Jonah sang a song in the night and God delivered him.

Job did the same thing when he was stripped of his health, wealth, and family. He responded by saying, "Though he slay me, yet will I trust in him" (Job 13:15). And the Bible says that God restored unto Job twice what he had before.

It was the same with Paul and Silas in a Philippian jail. Although they were chained to prison guards, at midnight these two men sang a song that opened prison doors. It would have been easy for them to have cried out about the unfairness of their punishment. After all, they had done nothing to warrant it. They had left their homes for the sake of the gospel. They had sacrificed much. They could easily have slipped into resentment. But the Bible says, "About midnight Paul and Silas were praying and singing hymns to God, and the other prisoners were listening to them. Suddenly there was such a violent earthquake that the foundations of the prison were shaken. At once all the prison doors flew open, and everybody's chains came loose" (Acts 16:25-26).

Here are the keys that unlock the door: praise and thanksgiving. They will set us free. You say, "But I don't have anything to praise God about." Well, we don't praise God for what He gives us; we praise him for who He is.

Had Paul and Silas been like a lot of modernday disciples, scripture would have read, "At midnight Paul and Silas whined and whimpered and questioned God." But instead, like Jonah, they praised the Lord in the midst of adversity, and God set them free.

Could this be the very point at which our own deliverance is waiting? Praise is the garment we must put on as believers when we have a spirit of despair (Isaiah 61:3). Is it dark in your life? Do you feel as though you are in prison at midnight? Are you in the belly of a fish? Do not allow yourself to wallow in self-pity. Begin to praise the Lord. When we sing a song in the night, when we praise the Lord in adversity, God hears and acts.

There is no more beautiful illustration of this than is found in 2 Chronicles:

> Listen, King Jehoshaphat and all who live in Judah and Jerusalem! This is what the Lord says to you: "Do not be afraid or discouraged because of this vast army. For the battle is not yours, but God's. Tomorrow march down against them. They will be climbing up by the Pass of Ziz, and you will find them at the end of the gorge in the Desert of Jeruel. You will not have to fight this battle. Take up your positions; stand firm and see the deliverance the Lord will give you, O Judah and Jerusalem. Do not be afraid; do not be discouraged. Go out to face them tomorrow, and the Lord will be with you." Jehoshaphat bowed with his face to the ground, and all the people of Judah and Jerusalem fell down in worship before the Lord. Then some Levites from the Kohathites and Korahites stood up and praised the Lord, the God of Israel, with a very loud voice. Early in the morning they left for the Desert of Tekoa. As they set out, Jehoshaphat stood and said, "Listen to me, Judah and the people of Jerusalem! Have faith in the Lord your God and you will be upheld; have faith in his prophets and you will be successful." After consulting the people, Jehoshaphat appointed men to sing to the Lord and to praise him for the splendor of his holiness as they went out at the head of the army, saying: "Give thanks to the Lord, for his love endures forever." As they began to sing and praise, the Lord set ambushes against the men of Ammon and Moab and Mount Seir who were invading Judah, and they were defeated (2 Chronicles 20: 15-22).

During the reign of King Jehoshaphat, the Ammonites and the Moabites came up against the Israelites. Jehoshaphat knew he was out-matched. What could he do? He marched and sang praises to God. In the hour of trial instead of cowering in fear he sang praises, and the outcome was glorious.

Are you in the fish's belly? Are you in the dark, confused, in despair and distress? Never give up. You cannot keep a good man, a man of praise, down.

Here is a good place to begin finding the will of God. The Bible says, "Give thanks in all circumstances, for this is God's will for you in Christ Jesus" (1 Thessalonians 5:18). Did you hear that? This is God's will. Our giving thanks is God's will. This does not necessarily say that we are to thank God *for* the fish's belly, but thank God *in* the fish's belly.

Our faith is proven by our thanksgiving. There is quite a difference between those who walk by sight and those who walk by faith. Those who walk by sight can sing songs of praise and thanksgiving only when deliverance has come. Anyone can do that. We get a new job and we give thanks. We get a good report from the doctor and we give praise and thanks. We make an important sale in our business and we give praise and thanks. But those who walk by faith choose to live in thanksgiving even in the midst of adversity. God says, "He who sacrifices thank offerings honors me, and he prepares the way so that I may show him the salvation of God" (Psalm 50:23).

IV. A MAN OF PERCEPTION

"But I, with a song of thanksgiving, will sacrifice to you. What I have vowed I will make good. Salvation comes from the Lord." And the Lord commanded the fish, and it vomited Jonah onto dry land (Jonah 2:9-10).

A casual reading of the text might cause us to pass over what Jonah said in the last part of 2:9: "Salvation comes from the Lord." It is God who delivers. As long as there are still a few strings for us to pull, deliverance can be traced to our own efforts. We are not saved because we deserve to be, or because we are good, or because we are moral, or because we are intelligent, or because we are talented, or because we are American. Salvation and deliverance are "of the Lord." Jonah finally perceived this. He was not only a man of prayer and purpose and praise; now he was a man of perception.

Jonah was saying, "It is out of my hands. There is nothing I can do." Jonah knew that only a loving God would take him back after the rebellion he had pursued. He knew that his deliverance had to be of the Lord.

God has a special way of bringing us to this point, doesn't he? When we are rebellious, he has a way of getting us to the place where we finally have to say, "Lord, it is out of my hands; there is nothing more I can do. Deliverance must come from you."

It will be a happy day when we stop trying to deliver ourselves and become men and women of prayer, purpose, praise, and perception, knowing that deliverance comes only from the Lord. Some of us are still in the fish's belly because we have never gotten to that place of understanding. Some of us have become men and women of prayer, calling to God in our distress. Some of us have become men and women of purpose, realizing that our disobedience wasn't worth it. Some of us have even thanked God for the hard experience, and have become men and women of praise. But all of that is not enough. We need to take the final step of acknowledging that deliverance is totally of the Lord and unless He comes through we are sunk. Jonah came to that place when finally he said, "I can't, but He can. Salvation is of the Lord."

The apostle Paul said, "For to me, to live is Christ and to die is gain" (Philippians 1:21). Until now in Jonah's pilgrimage, he had said, "For to me, to live is self."[4] How would you complete that sentence? For to me to live—is what? For to me to live is selfishness? For to me to live is business? For to me to live is pleasure? For to me to live is my boat? For to me to live is money? For to me to live is the kids? God did not keep Jonah down there one second longer than it took to get Jonah to repent and acknowledge his dependency on a loving God.

I really appreciate the final verse of this chapter. God spoke to the fish, and out came Jonah. The way out of a fish's belly is to be a person of prayer, purpose, praise, and perception. And the word of the Lord will come to you a second time.

Thank God He is the God of the second chance.
   Thank God that you cannot keep a good man down.

---

1. Blair, J. Allen. 1963. *Jonah.* Neptune NJ: Loizeaux Brothers, Inc., p. 65.
2. Hawkins, O. S. 1982. *Clues to a Successful Life.* Nashville TN: Broadman Press, p. 94.
3. Kendall, R. T. 1978. *Jonah.* London: Hodder & Stoughton, p. 129.
4. Blair, *Jonah*, p. 72.

CHAPTER FIVE
What Can One Person Do?
Jonah 3:1-10

I. CORRECT OUR WAYS
   A. Seize Our Opportunities
   B. Sense Our Obligation

II. CHANGE OUR WORLD
   A. Faith
   B. Fasting
   C. Forsaking
   D. Forgiveness

History is replete with stories of what one solitary person can do to change his or her world. Ask Moses what one person can do; after hearing God speak from a burning bush, he went back to Egypt and became the emancipator of his people. Ask Nehemiah what one man can do; after having heard the report of the broken-down walls of Jerusalem, he left his civil service job and went back to lead the rebuilding of the broken walls. What can one man do? Ask William Wilberforce of Great Britain; virtually singlehandedly he brought an end to slavery in that nation a century ago.

What can one person do? Look at Jonah. Remember, he had previously failed, and no doubt some people were saying that God could never use him again. But one of the greatest revivals in history came to the city of Nineveh, and it all began with Jonah, with one man who repented and got right with God.

The truth is, you are important. You could be the key to revival in your home, your church, your city, your nation, your world. Some people may look around the office in which they work, seeing all the others who live such ungodly lives, and wonder what could they ever do in such an environment. What can one man or woman do in such a setting? Young people at school, overwhelmed when everyone else is going the way of the world, ask themselves that same question, "What can one person do?"

Let's look at Jonah and continue using him as our example as we see what one man can do. We begin by noting that we cannot change our world until we correct our ways.

I. CORRECT OUR WAYS

Then the word of the Lord came to Jonah a second time. "Go to the great city of Nineveh and proclaim to it the message I give you." Jonah obeyed the word of the Lord and went to Nineveh. Now Nineveh was a very important city—a visit required three days. On the first day, Jonah started into the city. He proclaimed: "Forty more days and Nineveh will be overturned" (Jonah 3:1-4).

Some of us have forgotten that we have the ability to correct our ways. How?

A. Seize Our Opportunities

First, we can seize our opportunities. Jonah seized the opportunity of a second chance. It is one thing to be delivered and washed up on shore. However, merely being ejected from the fish will not solve all our problems. It is another thing to have a second chance and do something about it. God doesn't just deliver us; He gives us a second chance. How regrettable it is that some persons never correct their ways because they do not seize the opportunity of the second chance.

I am sure that between chapters 2 and 3 of the book of Jonah, the main character lived in a state of wondering if God would ever use him again. Certainly God was under no obligation to do so. Trying to put myself in Jonah's place, I suppose nothing would be more painful than the feeling of uselessness, the fear, that God had put me on the shelf, that haunting gnawing that because of a previous mistake God would never use me again. What a feeling of frustration and failure I would have. But listen to the word of God: "The word of the Lord came to Jonah a second time." What a comfort it is to realize that the best of God's servants have made foolish mistakes, but were used again. God is not through with me yet, and He is not through with you yet.

The Bible is the continuous record of God coming the second time with another opportunity, and of men and women seizing that opportunity. In the garden of Eden, God said, "You are free to eat from any tree in the garden; but you must not eat from the tree of the knowledge of good and evil, for when you eat of it, you will surely die" (Genesis 2:16-17). As we all know, Adam and Eve ate of the forbidden tree. They fell. And what did God do? He came a second time in the cool of the day to mend the broken relationship.

God always comes a second time. What if the first time you heard the gospel of Jesus Christ and his love for you was also the last time? The chances are that few of us would have come to know him in the free pardoning of sin. Many of us are in the family of God today because the word of the Lord came to us a second time, or a third, or a fourth, or a tenth time. Perhaps some reader today has gone her or his own way in life. Like Jonah you have disobeyed God and gotten out of his will. Let me assure you that our God is the God of the second chance, but it is not enough that He provides the second chance. We must seize the opportunity when it is presented.

Some say sadly, "I've missed God's best for me." Before we take off on a guilt trip like that, we ought to remember that we all have missed God's best for us. God's best was in the garden. Ever since the fall of man, God has been the God of the second chance. We all have sinned, gone our own way, and are in need of a second chance.

We read of many in the Bible who took advantage of the second opportunity. What about Lot? Lot was a city boy. He grabbed the best land with the brightest lights. But he seized the opportunity for a second chance and repented before Sodom was destroyed.

And do not forget David, the king who had it all going for him and thought he could cover his sin when his lust had gotten the best of him. He seized his opportunity for a second chance, repented, and went on to the most effective years of his life.

And there was Samson, rugged and handsome, who had so much going for him until he fell into sin. But in his last days God gave him a second chance and he corrected his ways and seized the opportunity.

Many of us can identify with Simon Peter. Peter denied our Lord the night He needed him the most. Later Jesus met him on the shore and Peter corrected his ways by seizing the opportunity of a second chance.

And on and on we can go throughout the Bible. If God could use men like that again, He certainly can use us again. He can use us if we correct our ways by seizing the opportunity of the second chance.

Some sense the opportunity of the second chance but never seize it. We have no right to assume that God will go on giving us opportunity after opportunity to get right with him. God is giving that second chance today. Nothing we have done is unforgivable, with the exception of our continued refusal to receive his grace.

What can one person do? We can begin by correcting our ways. How? By seizing the opportunity of a second chance.

The second chance came Jonah's way and he responded in obedience. Some of us wonder why we do not obey God and, the truth is, we do not obey him because we do not trust him. If we really trusted him, we would obey him. But a step farther back to the root shows us that we do not trust him because we do not know him in the intimacy of Father and child. If we really knew him, we would trust him. Jonah had gotten to know God again in the belly of the fish and he trusted him. Obedience naturally followed. When the word of the Lord came a second time, Jonah obeyed. I believe that when he moved in obedience he began to anticipate what was going to happen. I can almost see him now, marching confidently in the power of the Holy Spirit to Nineveh, forgiven and grateful for a second chance.

Jonah had heard from God. What moved him now was the word of God. What moves you? Some of us wonder why God never seems to use us. The answer should be obvious. The real lesson here is that God gives us orders and when God gives us orders, He sticks with them. When God said "go" to Jonah, He meant it. God came a second time with the same message: "Go to Nineveh." Could it be that God has told us to go and we have said no.

Do you see it? Obedience arises from faith and trust. Jonah had learned a great lesson in the depths. He had learned that if there were no valleys, there would be no mountaintops. He had learned obedience.

Jonah also repented of his ways. Before, God had said, "Go to Nineveh," and Jonah went in the opposite direction. Now he had changed his mind and was enroute to Nineveh. That is repentance.

Repentance is a change of mind that is always evidenced in three ways. First, there is a change of attitude, a change intellectually. Repentance begins with a change of mind. Second, there is a change of affections, a change emotionally, a change of the heart. Third, there is a change of action, a change in one's volition, one's will. If we genuinely change our minds, our hearts will change too and our actions will follow.

The most obvious biblical illustration of repentance is found in the fifteenth chapter of Luke's gospel in the story of the prodigal son. First, the prodigal underwent a change of attitude. The Bible says he "came to himself." He changed his mind. Then what happened? He had a change of affections. He said, "How many of my father's hired servants have bread enough and to spare and I am perishing with hunger?" His heart was changed. After having a change of attitude and a change of affection, he had a change of action. His will was changed. He said, "I will arise and go to my father." In Luke

15:20 the Bible says, "He got up and went to his father."

And so it was with the prodigal prophet Jonah. He was now in the will of God. Could it be that revival is just waiting for us to get in the will of God? I do not know where Nineveh is for you, but I know that God will "make known to you the path of life." There you will find fullness of joy. There is something a lot more fun than being on a Mediterranean cruise to Tarshish, and that is going to Nineveh in the will of God. The truly happy people of this world are not necessarily those who look like it on the outside, but those who are happy on the inside by being in the will of God.

B. Sense Our Obligation

How do we correct our ways? First, we can seize our opportunities; second, we can sense our obligations. God again told Jonah to go to the city of Nineveh and "proclaim to it the message I give you." Jonah went to Nineveh and preached God's message: "Forty more days and Nineveh will be overturned."

As God's messengers, we are obliged to take his word and not our own to the world. When we take our own views, we may persuade people to believe us, but when we take God's word the Holy Spirit persuades them to believe him. It is interesting to note in Jonah 3:5 that the Ninevites "believed God." A lot of God's preachers today are out of his will by preaching their own messages instead of God's. Some see the Bible from the viewpoint of the world, and others see the world from the viewpoint of the Bible. Jonah's message was not some compromising, watered-down, mamby-pamby, candy-coated sermonette. No, he now sensed his obligation to be faithful to the word. He spoke the truth of God's word. Paul later put it like this: "For I received from the Lord what I also passed on to you" (1 Corinthians 11:23). Paul also said, "When I preach the gospel, I cannot boast, for I am compelled to preach. Woe to me if I do not preach the gospel!" (1 Corinthians 9:16).

Jonah could have gone to Nineveh and sought out the right contacts and said all the right things. He could have influenced others through his personality so that just the right peo-

ple would recommend him with flowing words. And who
knows? Perhaps he would have landed a position as chaplain
to the king. But Nineveh would never have come to repentance. How sad it is today that so many preachers are interested only in titles and positions. This is why there are a lot
of dead churches who are pastored by men who pull all the
strings denominationally and politically—and revival never
comes.

Preaching that does not bring men and women face to face
with their sin and with God's will for their lives never produces
repentance. The preacher who refuses to renounce sin, who
seeks to make others feel comfortable in their sin, is often cov-
ering his own. I know of a preacher who prides himself in not
making his people feel guilty. He preaches about soothing
things, good things, popular things. Jonah sensed his obligations and sounded forth the frightening message from God.

That message certainly was not a popular one. It certainly
would not make people feel comfortable. Pastors who sense
the obligation of being faithful to God's word are those who
love their people too much not to tell them the truth from
God's word. We must "preach the message that God has given
us." The greatest revival in the history of the world came to
Nineveh because Jonah preached God's message, and not
what the people wanted to hear.

We see here the need for a delicate balance in the preaching
of God's word. Yes, there is a second chance. Yes, we have a
redemptive message in the gospel. Yes, God can forgive and
cleanse the past. But the teaching of these truths must be
done in such a way that anyone who is contemplating a life of
sin would not say, "I'll go out and sin and God will forgive me."
If anyone says that or believes that, he or she knows nothing
of the grace of God and of repentance.

This message cannot be preached unless we ourselves are
correcting our ways. The only message with power is the message that is preached with a pure heart by persons of clean
hands. All else is sounding brass and tinkling cymbals.

There do not seem to be enough preachers today who sense
their obligation to the word of God. Some men are soothingly,

softly, whispering, "Believe, believe, believe." That kind of preaching is popular today. Do you know why? It calls for no change of lifestyle. It is foreign to the preaching that brings revival. It has forgotten the word *repentance.*

Woe to the preacher who does not warn his people that judgment is coming. We are not going to get away with sin. Each of us is going to stand before God, and if any of us says, "I'll live however I want because I am under the blood," we should examine our own salvation. Many have been living a lie for years; and all the while, judgment is coming. God has a limit to his patience with us.

We do not choose what we preach as ministers of the gospel. We do not have a choice of what we preach week by week. There are times in my study when I am absolutely overcome when I sense that God has spoken to me through his word for our people. Pulpits are not private platforms to espouse personal philosophies or political views. The only preaching God honors is "the message that I give you." In my pulpit I preach from the Bible for two reasons. First, I am not smart enough to preach anything else. If I were to preach on social issues, there are sociologists in my congregation who would know far more about them than I. If I were to preach on political issues, there are politicians who would know more than I do in that field. Second, I am too smart to preach anything else because I know that God blesses his word and it will not return void.

What is this message God has called us to proclaim? Paul said it best: "Preach the Word; be prepared in season and out of season; correct, rebuke and encourage—with great patience and careful instruction" (2 Timothy 4:2). This is the word of God that is "useful for teaching, rebuking, correcting and training in righteousness" (2 Timothy 3:16).

There is no limit to what can happen in a fellowship when we preach the message God gives us. God says, "So is my word that goes out from my mouth: it will not return to me empty, but will accomplish what I desire and achieve the purpose for which I sent it" (Isaiah 55:11). "The grass withers and the flowers fall, but the word of our God stands forever" (Isaiah 40:8).

Note Jonah's message: "Forty more days and Nineveh will be overturned." God could have leveled Nineveh without any warning. But in his love and mercy He warned them first. He gave them time to repent. He gave them a final opportunity.

Nineveh would be overturned. The judgment of God was coming. The wrath of God was enroute. Here was a message from God, a message of wrath and judgment wrapped in a message of love and mercy. We find the same ideas in John 3:16: "For God so loved the world that he gave his one and only Son, that whoever believes in him shall not perish but have eternal life." Where is the message of love? "For God so loved the world." Where is the message of judgment? "Whoever believes in him shall not perish."

This sermon that brought such a mighty revival contained only one sentence: "Forty more days and Nineveh will be overturned" (Jonah 3:4). It shows us that God is serious about his word and we must not be ashamed to preach it. Jonah went to Nineveh more concerned about being faithful to God and the message he was to preach than he was in getting the key to the city from the mayor. A lot of us today are more interested in being accepted as "one of the boys" than we are in delivering an uncompromising message of judgment that calls for repentance. The reason some ministers do not preach God's message of God's judgment and wrath today is they are ashamed in this modern world to admit they believe in hell and judgment. But there is a greater tragedy than that. The reason some others do not preach God's message of judgment and wrath today is that they are ashamed to admit they do *not* believe in hell and judgment.

One of the devil's foremost lies today is that the message of judgment scares people away from church. In our plastic society, men and women are wanting to know the truth. Growing churches are churches that proclaim the "message God gives them." The folly of this present church age is that many think they can attract people by boasting that they are too progressive to believe in such things as judgment and wrath. Sadly, their churches are empty and dead. When we read the history of revivals we find that they were all born out of preaching about the wrath of God.

However, I'm not just pointing a finger at those of us who are preachers. Mostly, it is lay men and women who have not seized their opportunities and sensed their obligations. We have not changed our world because we have not corrected our ways. What can one person do? We have seen what one person can do in a negative sense. A Madalyn Murray O'Hair can get prayer out of the public schools almost singlehandedly because she set her mind to it. Would to God that all Christians were as committed to Christ as she is to atheism.

We are putting a lot of blame on churches for the decline of influence of Christianity in American life today, but may I ask, "Where have the Christian lawyers been?" Where have they been while liberal forces have made the First Amendment to be what it was never intended to be? Where have the Christian lawyers been while liberal organizations have stripped nearly every moral fiber that this nation was built on and turned the tables on the intent of our founding fathers? Where have the Christian attorneys been?

Many Christians have fallen into the trap of universalism. Some time ago I received a fundraising letter from a leader of a major church-state separation organization. This Baptist minister was accusing conservative Christians of trying to "Christianize America." He was attempting to raise funds to head off their influence. I was shocked and appalled. I am unapologetically trying to Christianize America. Why? Because the Bible still says, "Salvation is found in no one else, for there is no other name under heaven given to men by which we must be saved" (Acts 4:12). Jesus says, "I am the way and the truth and the life. No one comes to the Father except through me" (John 14:6). In fact we should not simply be trying to Christianize America, we should be trying to Christianize the world. This is the commission our Lord has given us.

Where have the Christian educators been? We are watching our education system crumbling at the hands of humanists. Christian teachers in public schools are no more allowed to espouse Christian morals and virtues in the classroom than teachers are in Russia. They are just as banned by law from doing so as schools in the Soviet Union. On the day of the horrible explosion of the shuttle Challenger, Billy Graham made a classic statement to the media. He said, "America is stunned. It has caused us to pray. Students are praying in classrooms all over America today where it has been voted illegal to pray."

Where have the Christian doctors been? Abortion has taken millions of innocent lives while judges and politicians argue over when life begins. God made it plain in his word. He said, "Before you were formed in the womb, I knew you and called you by name."

Where have the Christian businessmen and women been? Our cities have sunk to a level of debauchery and degeneration that would make Sodom and Gomorrah blush.

The question returns to us, "What can one person do?" We can correct our ways and then we can change our world.

II. CHANGE OUR WORLD

The Ninevites believed God. They declared a fast, and all of them, from the greatest to the least, put on sackcloth. When the news reached the king of Nineveh, he rose from his throne, took off his royal robes, covered himself with sackcloth and sat down in the dust. Then he issued a proclamation in Nineveh: "By the decree of the king and his nobles: Do not let any man or beast, herd or flock, taste anything; do not let them eat or drink. But let man and beast be covered with sackcloth. Let everyone call urgently on God. Let them give up their evil ways and their violence. Who knows? God may yet relent and with compassion turn from his fierce anger so that we will not perish." When God saw what they did and how they turned from their evil ways, he had compassion and did not bring upon them the destruction he had threatened (Jonah 3:5-10).

It is amazing what happened when one man got right with God. When one man, Jonah, corrected his ways, he changed his world. The whole city of Nineveh came to God.

A. Faith

In Nineveh there came faith. "The Ninevites believed God."
The Bible says, "Faith comes by hearing the message, and the
message is heard through the word of Christ" (Romans 10:17).
Jonah went to Nineveh and delivered God's word. They heard,
and the result was that they "believed God." It does not say
they "believed Jonah." No, "They believed God." This should
be the aim and end of all preaching, that men and women
believe God. These people of Nineveh believed that God was
speaking to them through his prophet. It never occurred to
them that this was Jonah's philosophy. He was nothing more
than God's delivery boy with God's message, and consequently
they "believed God."

I wonder if it could be that men and women in our offices,
neighborhoods, and schools are wanting to believe, but God's
problem is with us. Imagine, God wants to use us to bring *faith*
to others.

When men and women get right with God, the lost are
attracted. Let a Jonah get right with God and the entire city
of Nineveh gets saved. Let a woman at a well drink of "living
water" and she brings out the town of Sychar to the Lord
Jesus. Let the disciples tarry in an upper room and three thousand people will be saved at Pentecost. One of the ways to
know if revival has come is that it always results in a multitude
of people being swept into the kingdom. Revival leads a man,
as it did Jonah, to go to the lost, and God moves in with great
power. One person can be the spark that leads multitudes to
the Lord Jesus. Jonah brought faith to Nineveh.

B. Fasting

The Ninevites combined prayer with fasting. Spiritual matters
consumed their interest. Here is a test of genuine revival. It
involves a change of heart. Our Lord himself said that some
things happen only as a result of prayer and fasting. I seriously
doubt that there is any great moving of God's Spirit in revival
that has not been born out of prayer and fasting.

The first thing they did after they believed God was to proclaim a fast. Fasting seems to be one of the lost words in our Christian vocabulary today. *Fasting* can be defined as the voluntary denial of food in order that the face of God might be sought in earnest, definite, persistent, and believing prayer. Fasting and prayer are inseparable.

Why should we fast? Look at the Ninevites. All through the Bible, people have fasted when they met God. Do you remember Moses in the wilderness?

> Then the Lord said to Moses, "Write down these words, for in accordance with these words I have made a covenant with you and with Israel." Moses was there with the Lord forty days and forty nights without eating bread or drinking water. And he wrote on the tablets the words of the covenant—the Ten Commandments" (Exodus 34:27-28).

Later the Israelites were involved in a civil war between the sons of Israel and the sons of Benjamin. The Bible records, "Then the Israelites, all the people, went up to Bethel, and there they sat weeping before the Lord. They fasted that day until evening and presented burnt offerings and fellowship offerings to the Lord" (Judges 20:26). Later when Saul died, it is said of David that he and "all the men with him took hold of their clothes and tore them. They mourned and wept and fasted until evening for Saul and his son Jonathan" (2 Samuel 1:11-12). When David's boy was sick, the Bible says he "pleaded with God for the child. He fasted and went into his house and spent the night lying on the ground. The elders of his household stood beside him to get him up from the ground, but he refused, and he would not eat any food with them" (2 Samuel 12:16-17). When Nehemiah heard of the reproach of the broken-down walls of Jerusalem he said, "I sat down and wept. For some days I mourned and fasted and prayed before the God of heaven" (Nehemiah 1:4). The Jewish Queen Esther said, "Go, gather together all the Jews who are in Susa, and fast for me. Do not eat or drink for three days, night or day" (Esther 4:16).

Jesus fasted. He was "led by the Spirit into the desert to be tempted by the devil. After fasting forty days and forty nights, he was hungry" (Matthew 4:1-2). The early church fasted. "While they were worshiping the Lord and fasting, the Holy Spirit said, 'Set apart for me Barnabas and Saul for the work to which I have called them.' So after they had fasted and prayed, they placed their hands on them and sent them off" (Acts 13:2-3). In the early church "Paul and Barnabas appointed elders for them in each church and, with prayer and fasting, committed them to the Lord in whom they had put their trust" (Acts 14:23).

Why is it that so many today who seek after God totally neglect this truth of scripture? Many churches today make their major decisions by their bank accounts and economic forecasts. Whatever became of prayer and fasting? Why should we fast? We should fast because it is practiced all through the word of God and it is God's plan for bringing things to pass in the life of individuals and churches.

Another question should be: "When should we fast?" Look at the Ninevites. We should fast when our walk with God needs to be deepened and our faith restored. We should fast when victories need to be won. We should fast when decisions need to be made. In Antioch they fasted when they sent out the missionaries. We should fast when power needs to be secured. We should fast when revival needs to be experienced.

Where should we fast? Should we fast privately or publicly? There are needs for public fasts. We see it here in the book of Jonah, when the king ordered the fast. However, I believe that our basic need today is for private fasting. In the sermon on the mount, Jesus said:

> When you fast, do not look somber as the hypocrites do, for they disfigure their faces to show men they are fasting. I tell you the truth, they have received their reward in full. But when you fast, put oil on your head and wash your face, so that it will not be obvious to men that you are fasting, but only to your Father, who is unseen; and your Father, who sees what is done in secret, will reward you (Matthew 6:16-18).

Those in the fellowship of believers we call the First Baptist
Church of Fort Lauderdale will be quick to tell you that major
decisions are made only after prayer and fasting.

C. Forsaking

There was also forsaking. "Let them give up their evil ways
and their violence." When the people heard the message God
had delivered through Jonah, conviction of the Holy Spirit set
in. Although they were living wicked, immoral, licentious, sin-
ful lives, then there came faith and fasting, followed by a forsaking.

It is interesting to note that "all of them, from the greatest
to the least" fasted and forsook their evil ways. Sometimes
people try to convince us that the message of God's wrath and
judgment is only for the unlearned and uneducated. Some sit
comfortable in their padded pews with their five-hundred-dol-
lar suits looking down their liturgical noses at those who are
so religiously naive that they accept the message of God's judgment. In Nineveh *all* the people believed.

All human beings are the same in that all have sinned, and
all have a part of them that will live forever. Repentance is a
universal need. In fact, the one who took the lead was the
greatest of all, the king of Nineveh. It was personal sin from
which each of them turned. It is one thing to talk and pray
about the sins of others, but it is another thing to come before
God and say "Are *my* hands clean? Is *my* heart pure?"

Herein lies real revival. It is in repentance. The Ninevites
changed their minds and "believed God." Consequently, this
changed their hearts and they called a fast. And this changed
their volition; they gave up their evil ways. They proved it by
their works. This was genuine repentance, a forsaking.

Some people are not sure what repentance is today. Some
think it is remorse, being sorry for one's sin. Remorse may
lead to repentance, but remorse is not repentance. The rich
young ruler "went away sorrowful" but did not repent.

Others think repentance is regret, wishing our deeds had
not happened. Many persons who regret their sin have never

JONAH 3:1-10   98

repented. Pontius Pilate is the most obvious biblical example. Many today substitute regret for repentance and fool themselves in the process.

Others think repentance is resolve; that is, they decide to do better in their own efforts and strength. But resolve is not repentance.

Still others think repentance is reform, turning over a new leaf. That is what Judas tried to do. After betraying our Lord for thirty pieces of silver, he went back to the temple and tried to give the money back. He went to the wrong people. There are many who have tried to substitute reform for repentance.[1]

Repentance is a change of mind which results in a change of heart which results in a change of action. We see it plainly here in the life of the Ninevites.

What can one person do? Look at Jonah. Does anyone want to influence a nation? Revival in Nineveh started with one man. It spread to the people, and they in turn influenced the leadership. There is a sense in which most leaders are really followers. When enough people are moved, we can reach to the top echelons. This is why it is so important for the church to correct its way and begin to change its world. It is vital today for the church to take the message God has given us and become salt and light in the world instead of simply in the church. We can change our world as Jonah changed Nineveh. We could become a place of faith and fasting and forsaking. Revival can affect the whole world.

D. Forgiveness

"When God saw what they did and how they turned from their evil ways, he had compassion and did not bring upon them the destruction he had threatened" (Jonah 3:10). This was the result of it all.

Does God repent? Does God change his mind? "Every good and perfect gift is from above, coming down from the Father of the heavenly lights, who does not change like shifting shadows" (James 1:17). "I the Lord do not change. So you, O descendants of Jacob, are not destroyed" (Malachi 3:6). "God

is not a man, that he should lie, nor the Son of Man, that he should change his mind. Does he speak and then not act? Does he promise and not fulfill?" (Numbers 23:19).
and then not act? Does he promise and not fulfill?" (Numbers 23:19).

Other verses in the Bible say such things as: "The Lord was grieved that he had made man on the earth, and his heart was filled with pain" (Genesis 6:6). "Then the Lord relented and did not bring on his people the disaster he had threatened" (Exodus 32:14). Perhaps the most familiar is found in 2 Kings 20:1-6.

In those days Hezekiah became ill and was at the point of death. The prophet Isaiah son of Amoz went to him and said, "This is what the Lord says: Put your house in order, because you will die; you will not recover." Hezekiah turned his face to the wall and prayed to the Lord, "Remember, O Lord, how I have walked before you faithfully and with wholehearted devotion and have done what is good in your eyes." And Hezekiah wept bitterly. Before Isaiah had left the middle court, the word of the Lord came to him: "Go back and tell Hezekiah, the leader of my people, 'This is what the Lord, the God of your father David, says: I have heard your prayer and seen your tears; I will heal you. On the third day from now you will go up to the temple of the Lord. I will add fifteen years to your life. And I will deliver you and this city from the hand of the king of Assyria. I will defend this city for my sake and for the sake of my servant David.'"

So back to the question: Does God change his mind? The answer is *no* and the answer is *yes*.[2] In his character, the answer is *no*, for He is holy and just and unchangeable. In his mercy, the answer is *yes*, for He turns his face to any seeking sinner, saying, "Draw nigh to me and I will draw nigh to you." God repented of the punishment He said He would bring to Nineveh when they repented of the evil they had done.

While preaching some time ago at Moody Bible Institute in Chicago, I saw this illustrated while walking from my hotel to the school to preach. Those who have visited the Windy City know that it is not called that for nothing. Anyone who has walked the streets of downtown Chicago knows that the wind as it comes off Lake Michigan blows like few other places in the world. I started my walk from the hotel against a strong wind. The wind was so strong that it seemed to hold me back as I tried to walk. I literally had to lean into it. I had not gotten very far when I realized I had left my notebook in the hotel room and needed to go back for it. When I turned and went in the opposite direction the same wind helped me along the journey. In fact, it almost blew me over. Now, the wind didn't change, but I changed in relation to it. F. B. Meyer said that is how some of us find ourselves in relation to the will of God. When we are out of his will, the wind of the Holy Spirit blows against us. We repent, turn around, change directions and then the wind of the Holy Spirit helps us along. God never changes. What happens is that we change in our relationship to him.

"God saw what they did," and He sent a mighty revival. The Ninevites gave up their evil ways. A lot of people today want to see revival but too few want to pay the price. What can one person do? It is clear that one reason God sent revival to Nineveh was that Jonah experienced revival in his heart. He was the key. You could be the key. Perhaps there is a Jonah reading these words, some person whom God is convicting to correct his or her ways and thus to become an agent of revival. How thankful we should be that our God is a God of the second chance.

What can one person do? Ask Jeremiah Lamphier. He lived in the 1850s when America was in a sad and sickened state. There was great luxury on the part of a few and great poverty on the part of many. The crime rate soared. Violence was common. City streets were unsafe. Free love was espoused by some and home and family seemed to be on the verge of collapse. Economic instability haunted the nation and unemployment raged out of control. Corruption and injustice shamelessly walked hand in hand in high places. The slavery question and racial divisions separated family and friends.

Many wondered if the "land of the free and the home of the brave" was not writing the last chapter of its history.

In 1857 Jeremiah Lamphier bore a tremendous burden for revival. He called on a handful of Christians to meet with him in a location on Fulton Street in New York for a prayer meeting in behalf of revival. He arrived at the appointed place on September 23, 1857, and was later joined by five others.

That inauspicious meeting was the beginning of a mighty prayer meeting from which dozens like it were launched across the country. It wasn't long before businessmen were closing their businesses and joining in prayer meetings to beseech God on behalf of their beloved country. Many were converted at those prayer meetings.

Throughout the land a divine fire broke out and white-haired penitents knelt with little children to receive Christ. Whole families of Jews were converted to their true messiah. Hardened infidels were melted, some being led to Christ by the testimonies of children. Some of the most amazing aspects of this revival were recorded in only a few little-known accounts. Its blessing was not confined to land; the Spirit literally moved on the face of the waters. Vessel after vessel arriving in New York harbor would come under the same tale of a mysterious conviction breaking out among the crewmen. Entire crews would find Christ at sea as they entered the atmosphere of the harbor.

Day after day the prayer meetings continued. It is estimated that during the months of the revival's greatest intensity, no less than fifty thousand persons a week were swept into the kingdom of God. Conservative estimates claim that more than a million people met Jesus Christ as savior in less than a twelve-month span as revival spread.[3] What can one person do? It all began when Jeremiah Lamphier corrected his ways and set out to change his world.

My cry today is: "Lord, do it again! As you did in the days of Lamphier, do it again!"

Is it now time? When the Bible has been laid aside as an error-filled and worn-out book of antiquity, while humanistic philosophies are being taught instead, is not our only hope genuine revival? When the heart of the church in many quarters has turned to stone, when the pulpit has become a dispensary of worldly philosophies, when our educational systems seem like citadels of unprincipled corruption and forthright atheism, is it not time to pray, "Lord, do it again as you did in the days of old?" Is it not time for the people of God to barrage heaven with cries for revival?

When old-fashioned evangelistic methods, once openly espoused, are condemned as crude and manipulative, and the altar call after hellfire-and-judgment preaching is denounced as a fear tactic, is it not time to cry out to God for a return to him?

When we see our nation sinking rapidly into the quicksands of immorality and insensitivity, with a seeming inability to call ourselves to arms, we should cry, "Lord visit us again with your sovereign power!" When from television, newspapers, and other public media, we hear the raucous cries of a thousand voices calling our children to lifestyles of godlessness, we should be moved to pray, "Lord, do it again, 'Will you not revive us again, that your people may rejoice in you?'" (Psalm 85:6).

When we see churches settling down to tolerate comfortably a declining civilization and adjusting their demands to accommodate indifference, we should know it is time for real revival. Nothing else will do.

When we see Christians pitifully struggling with half-hearted zeal to regain their first love, seeking to nurse a quiet desperation within their breasts, we know that revival is the only answer.

But most of all, when we imagine we can hear our savior, who wept over Jerusalem, weeping over this sin-cursed earth, we should be moved to pray with Isaiah, "Oh, that you would rend the heavens and come down" (Isaiah 64:1).

What can one person do? Look at what Jonah did.

---

1. Hawkins, O. S. 1984. *Where Angels Fear to Tread*. Nashville TN: Broadman Press, pp. 84-86.

2. Kendall, R. T. 1978. *Jonah.* London: Hodder & Stoughton, p. 203.
3. Hawkins, O. S. 1980. *When Revival Comes.* Nashville TN: Broadman Press, p. 32.

CHAPTER SIX
Warts and All
Jonah 4:1-11

I. THE DESTRUCTIVE RESULTS OF RESENTMENT
   A. Destroys Our Peace
   B. Diverts Our Purpose
   C. Diminishes Our Productiveness
   D. Distorts Our Perspective

II. THE DIVINE RESPONSE TO RESENTMENT
   A. Patience
   B. Protection
   C. Pardon

When Oliver Cromwell sat for the official portrait that would portray his appearance to future generations, he was said to have instructed the artist to paint him just as he saw him. He wanted no flattery to be involved in the portrait. In Cromwell's words, he instructed the artist to paint him "warts and all." Since that day the phrase "warts and all" has been used around the world, expressing the desire to give a true representation, to show all the defects as well as all the good points.

Jonah concludes the book that bears his name by showing us a picture of himself "warts and all." I have written several books, and at the conclusion of this one, I will soon begin the next. I have thought about Jonah as he wrote, and I am afraid,

had I been he, I would have been tempted to stop at the conclusion of chapter 3 with the mighty outpouring of God's Spirit
in revival on Nineveh. Great revival came and glory fell. But
Jonah doesn't end the book there. He goes on and adds the
fourth chapter to show us what he was really like. I believe he
did so in order that we might see ourselves in this chapter.

Jonah's "wart" was a spirit of resentment. He could not
stand the fact that the Ninevites had received the blessing of
God. Also, his own pride had been crushed, in that he had proclaimed, "Forty more days and Nineveh will be overturned,"
but God spared Nineveh. So Jonah went outside the city, sat
down filled with bitterness, and wished he were dead. One
would think that after he had obeyed the word of God, had
gone to Nineveh as God had commanded, and had seen the
glory he saw, he would be rejoicing. But no, he sat alone wallowing in anger. None of us is immune to this plague of resentment that ate at Jonah. It sometimes comes on us too, and
often it comes right after some victory—a time when we are
so prone to defeat. We are tempted to let yesterday's victories
suffice for today's commitment. We find ourselves sitting with
our chins cupped in our hands, wallowing in self-pity.

Jonah had lost his sense of perspective. He resented that
God forgave and blessed someone else. He began complaining
about little things. He was occupied with self. Listen to Jonah
4:3: "Now, O Lord, take away my life, for it is better for me to
die than to live." Note the personal pronouns.

We lose our concern for others and focus only on ourselves
when we fall prey to resentment. Jonah's sin of resentment is
revealed to us that we might see ourselves. Here we see not
only the destructive results of resentment, but the divine
response to it.

In this sovereign work of God which we call revival, we must
remember that we can not orchestrate it, nor can we duplicate
it, nor can we manipulate it. It is a genuine move of the Holy
Spirit. We cannot control him, but we can grieve him and
quench him. One of the primary ways the Spirit of God is
grieved and quenched in revival is by the sin of resentment.
Let's look at it and learn to deal with it.

I. The Destructive Results of Resentment

But Jonah was greatly displeased and became angry. He prayed to the Lord, "O Lord, is this not what I said when I was still at home? That is why I was so quick to flee to Tarshish. I knew that you are a gracious and compassionate God, slow to anger and abounding in love, a God who relents from sending calamity. Now, O Lord, take away my life, for it is better for me to die than to live." But the Lord replied, "Have you any right to be angry?" Jonah went out and sat down at a place east of the city. There he made himself a shelter, sat in its shade and waited to see what would happen to the city. Then the Lord God provided a vine and made it grow up over Jonah to give shade for his head to ease his discomfort, and Jonah was very happy about the vine. But at dawn the next day God provided a worm, which chewed the vine so that it withered. When the sun rose, God provided a scorching east wind, and the sun blazed on Jonah's head so that he grew faint. He wanted to die, and said, "It would be better for me to die than to live." But God said to Jonah, "Do you have a right to be angry about the vine?" "I do," he said, "I am angry enough to die." But the Lord said, "You have been concerned about this vine, though you did not tend it or make it grow. It sprang up overnight and died overnight. But Nineveh has more than a hundred and twenty thousand people who cannot tell their right hand from their left, and many cattle as well. Should I not be concerned about that great city?" (Jonah 4:1-11).

Resentment affects us in a damaging way.

A. Destroys Our Peace

Resentment destroys our peace. One would think that Jonah would have offered up a sacrifice of praise for the mighty outpouring of revival in Nineveh. Instead we read, "But Jonah was greatly displeased and became angry." The word *angry* means "to burn." Jonah was burning with anger. He was fuming. One of the first things which happens is that resentment destroys our peace and happiness. A grumpy Christian is no commendation for the gospel of the Lord Jesus Christ. Jesus came to give us life and to give it to us more abundantly. The evidence that one is really filled with the Spirit of God, and is abiding in revival, is "love, joy, and peace."

Jonah began to pray. It is quite an interesting prayer. It begins with the phrase "I knew." What a contrast that is to the apostle Paul who said, "I know." "Yet I am not ashamed, because I *know* whom I have believed, and am convinced that he is able to guard what I have entrusted to him for that day" (2 Timothy 1:12). To the Romans Paul wrote, "And we *know* that in all things God works for the good of those who love him, who have been called according to his purpose" (Romans 8:28). For Jonah it was simply a theory. He was living in the past. "I knew." For Paul it was a present confidence, "I know."[1]

What are you saying today? Are you saying, "I knew"? Or can you say, "I know"? Some of us are so full of resentment that the only thing we know about the peace of God is in the past tense. What a tragedy.

Jonah knew what it was to obey God, but he had no joy in that obedience. There are Christians like he was, those who obey out of sheer necessity but with no joy or peace. In his anger Jonah was totally blaming God. But the problem was not with God; it was with Jonah. Have you ever known anyone filled with resentment? Think about their countenance. Resentment destroys our peace.

B. Diverts Our Purpose

Resentment also diverts our purpose. Jonah was saying, "If I can't get my way, I don't want to live." He was down in the dumps. His pride was hurt because he felt that his ministry had been discredited. Now his resentment was diverting his purpose. He wanted to die. He was so self-centered that twice in this chapter he said, "I wish I were dead." Once he said it when he realized that what he had preached was not going to come about, and then he said it because of the "catastrophe" of losing his shade tree. The city of Nineveh had been saved and he was focusing on a vine. His purpose had been diverted through resentment. How many Christians have had that experience?

Had Jonah wanted to go outside the city and watch Nineveh burn? Perhaps he hoped a few of the people would come by and say, "You were right." Once, he had a purpose and he ful-filled it victoriously but no more. Now, his resentment had diverted his purpose and he was wishing he were dead.

The prophet Elijah had a similar experience and said the same thing a few decades earlier. Interestingly, Elijah's depres-sion also came right after a great victory. Immediately after defeating the prophets of Baal on mount Carmel, the Bible records:

> Elijah was afraid and ran for his life. When he came to
> Beersheba in Judah, he left his servant there, while he
> himself went a day's journey into the desert. He came to
> a broom tree, sat down under it and prayed that he might
> die. "I have had enough, Lord," he said. "Take my life; I
> am no better than my ancestors" (1 Kings 19:3-4).

Like Jonah, Elijah went out and sat down. Elijah sat not under a vine but under a juniper tree and, like Jonah, he requested to die. Remember, Elijah and Jonah were men who had been greatly used by God. But in allowing resentment to harbor in their hearts, they both not only had their peace destroyed but now their purposes were diverted. If it could happen to those mighty men of God in the Bible, surely it can happen to us if we are not on guard.

We see who Jonah was really interested in. He said, "It is better for *me* . . ." His resentment was causing him to make decisions on a what's-best-for-me basis. I wonder how many of God's people have had their purposes diverted because they did not get things their way and allowed resentment to well up within.

C. Diminishes Our Productiveness

Resentment also diminishes our productiveness. Twice in Jonah 4:5, the Bible tells us that Jonah "sat down." Once he had taken God's message through the streets of Nineveh, obeying the word of God and preaching God's message. He was so productive that a whole city came to God through his preaching. Now we see him merely sitting, half hoping Nineveh will fall so he can say, "I told you so."

How depressing these first few words are: "He went out of the city." If ever there was a time Jonah needed to be in Nineveh, it was during the days following the revival. Thousands had repented and were in need of guidance and teaching. Instead, they were left like sheep without a shepherd.

Some of us have "gone out of the city" in the past when we should have "gone in."[2] Some of us went out to escape the burdens and heartaches of others when we should have gone in to put an arm around them. But in our resentment and self-centeredness, our productiveness was diminished. Have you ever thought how much of our spiritual lives are taken up with sitting? Christians go to church and sit during the worship service; they sit in Sunday school class; they sit in Bible studies; they sit in choir practice; they sit in mission meetings; they sit in committee meetings; they sit in organization meetings. When we really think about it, much of what is done in most churches is little more than sitting!

Why did Jonah sit there? He wanted to see if God was going to destroy Nineveh. The city was rejoicing in the blessing of salvation and revival, but one person would not join in the rejoicing. Those who are filled with resentment are like that. They become touchy and quick to take offense. They find themselves a spot somewhere outside the city, and instead of rejoicing with the men and women who have been set free, they focus on themselves. Those filled with resentment are the ones who are always talking about their rights, and seldom, if ever, do they talk about their responsibilities. Why? Their productiveness and purpose are gone. Gone is their sense of mission. Gone is their sense of usefulness.

D. Distorts Our Perspective

Observing the destructive results of resentment, we see that it also distorts our perspective. Jonah was complaining about a vine and couldn't have cared less about the thousands of souls who had just repented of sin. For Jonah to sulk about a vine at a time like that was sheer folly.

We can shut the light of the sun out with a penny, if we hold it close enough to our eyes. A resentful person loses his or her sense of proportion and begins to pick at little things. We sometimes see it in families or businesses, and, regrettably, even in churches. Some churches with multimillion-dollar budgets have deacons and leaders who pick at items that make no difference whatsoever in kingdom advancement.

Jonah was not at all happy when thousands were saved, but he was "very happy about the vine." It is astounding how little it takes to make some people happy. What makes you happy? Some Christians rejoice only superficially when others are saved and are very happy when their personal needs are met. Jonah was "exceedingly happy" about his vine. Earlier he was "exceedingly angry" about revival. We can tell a lot about people by observing what makes them happy and what makes them sad, what makes them laugh and what makes them weep. When we get out of the will of God, our perspectives are distorted.

Jonah's happiness was determined by the changing conditions and circumstances of his life instead of by the unchanging God who controlled those conditions and circumstances. This is an easy trap in which we might fall if we are not careful. We will get more concerned over our vine than over people's souls. At this very moment as I am penning these words I am looking out my study window to the building across the parking lot that houses our clothing ministry. One particular man has caught my eye. He is pacing back and forth. He is unshaven and his hair is matted. He is like so many others who come by our church every day in downtown Fort Lauderdale. He is, in the words of pastor and author Jimmy Draper, "the shadow of a man he might have been." He is alone, with no one really to care if he arises tomorrow morning to beg through another day. Jonah did not care about the people of Nineveh. He was obsessed with his own comfort. But let's examine ourselves before we are too quick to condemn him.

Each of us should ask the question, "What is my vine?" In what do I trust and find joy? What makes me exceedingly happy? What blessings am I tempted to place above the divine blessor? If I am God's child and I start finding my greatest joy in the blessing, He might just send a worm to my vine to conform me to the image of Christ. In Jonah's case God prepared a worm and the vine was gone overnight. Some of us wonder why we used to be happy in the Lord Jesus and now we are angry. Some of us feel He has left us. Could it be that we started delighting more in the vine than in the Lord Jesus? Could it be that He sent a worm to show us it is not the temporal but the eternal that is really important?

Perhaps some of us find ourselves sitting beside Jonah on the hill overlooking our own Nineveh. Our vine is gone. That thing on which we centered our entire lives is gone. We can learn a lesson from Jonah: All is not lost. God is alive and He responds to our resentment with his love just as He did in Jonah's case. But Jonah was not nearly so bad off as some of us. At least he realized his plight and recorded it for posterity. Some of us will not be vulnerable enough to open up as Jonah did.

II. THE DIVINE RESPONSE TO RESENTMENT

A. Patience

God responds to our resentment with patience. After Jonah acted as he did, telling God that he wished he were dead, God patiently responded with a question, "Have you any right to be angry?" (Jonah 4:4). We often hear the phrase "the patience of Job," but here we see the patience of God. I am surprised that God did not slay Jonah on the spot when he requested it. But instead of taking Jonah's life, God began to work on him to bring him to himself. Our heavenly Father responds to our resentment with patience.

One moment Jonah was very happy about the vine, and the next moment he wanted to die. He took issue with God. He accused God of failing to keep his word. Jonah thought he knew everything. What audacity.

God could have said, "You are right to be angry." Some persons today suggest that this would have been the right reply; Jonah would go on his way and get over his resentment by being justified in his anger. A lot of counselors give that kind of advice. God could also have said, "You are wrong to be angry." A world of people today thrive on being told how wrong they are, and love to feel guilty.[3] But God did not condone and did not condemn.

Some of us need to see that if God did not give up on Jonah, He has not given up on us. I am thankful that God has been patient with me. It is wonderful to know that God still uses men and women who are frail and have failed. Some of us tend to have the idea that those who have seen the glory of God are somehow more free of problems than we are. I remember as a young Christian reading Jack Taylor's book *The Key to Triumphant Living*. It made an indelible impression on my life, as it has with scores of thousands over the years. I had never met Jack Taylor and thought to myself how he must live above difficulties and trials. Later, God caused our paths to cross and we have become lifelong friends. We have had wonderful times through the years vacationing and playing together as well as praying together. I found that he has as many struggles and shortcomings as I do.

There is a little of Jonah in all of us. We too have said things and done things as believers that could have caused God to finish us off, but He responded to us with patience. Is there anyone who needs a touch from him today?

> Standing somewhere in the shadows
> You'll find Jesus;
> He's the one who cares and understands.
> Standing somewhere in the shadows
> You'll find Jesus
> And you'll know him by the nail prints
> In his hands.

B. Protection

God also responds to our resentment with protection. God provided a vine to give shelter to Jonah and protection from the sun. God's intention with the vine was to comfort his prophet. He chose to use the protection of the vine to teach Jonah and us a valuable lesson: Soon the vine dies but God does not.

In Jonah's moment of need, he looked to the vine instead of God. How much better would it have been had he fixed his eyes on the Lord. How many of us, in a moment of need, have looked at our blessings instead of at the heavenly blessor, only to find them gone and all hope vanished? How much better had we too fixed our eyes on God.

Earlier the Lord had asked, "Do you have a right to be angry?" Now He probed deeper with the question, "Do you have a right to be angry about the vine?" (Jonah 4:9). Jeannette Clift George recently blessed us in a women's conference at our church. Many will remember that she played Corrie ten Boom in the motion picture *The Hiding Place*. She told us about wonderful times of fellowship she had with Corrie before her death. Corrie ten Boom along with her father and sister Betsy hid Jews from the Nazis in their clock shop in Holland. They were discovered and sent to a Nazi concentration camp. Horrible suffering followed, which resulted in Corrie's heart hardening toward God and a spirit of bitterness and resentment filling her life. Through it all, Betsy kept an open heart for God and spread the love of the Lord Jesus throughout the camp by her countenance and conversation. Betsy died in that Nazi prison, and Corrie heard God ask, "Do you have a right to be angry about the vine?" Upon her release, she picked up where Betsy had left off. Corrie ten Boom is in heaven today but she left us *The Hiding Place* and many other books telling of God's patience, protection, and pardon. "Do we have a right to be angry about the vine?" In our complaining, God has a right to ask that question, doesn't He?

There is a sense in which even the worm was there for Jonah's protection. That worm came when he needed it the most.

> There is a time for everything, and a season for every
> activity under heaven: a time to be born and a time to die,
> a time to plant and a time to uproot, a time to kill and a
> time to heal, a time to tear down and a time to build. A
> time to weep and a time to laugh, a time to mourn and a
> time to dance (Ecclesiastes 3:1-4).

Jonah needed the worm so that he might start looking to God
and not to the vine. Thank God for the vine. But thank God for
the worm too. Though we may not realize it, He continues to
protect us from ourselves by often removing our vines when
He sees they are occupying the center of our attention. The
very thing you may have considered your adversity, your
worm, may be there from God's protecting hand.

C. Pardon

God also responds to our resentment with pardon. Here is
amazing condescension! To think that God would come down
and reason with Jonah as He did. God is saying, "Jonah, have
you forgotten how I have dealt with you? I could have cut you
off when you sailed for Tarshish, but I didn't. I didn't have to
prepare a fish to protect you when you were thrown into the
sea, but I did. I responded to you with patience and protection
and now with pardon. Should I respond any differently to
those in Nineveh?"

   God was revealing to Jonah that since He was good to him
when he did not deserve it, why should He not be good to others who do not deserve it? He was trying to teach Jonah the
lesson Paul sought to teach the Ephesians.

> Do not grieve the Holy Spirit of God with whom you were
> sealed for the day of redemption. Get rid of all bitterness,
> rage and anger, brawling and slander, along with every
> form of malice. Be kind and compassionate to one anoth-
> er, forgiving each other, just as in Christ God forgave you
> (Ephesians 4:30-32).

As you read these words, are you suffering from resentment? If so, then you know that it destroys one's peace, diverts one's purpose, diminishes one's productiveness, and distorts one's perspective. Resentment is a sin and is to be dealt with as any other sin. It is to be confessed and forsaken.

The story ends without our ever knowing what happened. Did Jonah go on in his resentment to the bitter end? After all, when a book ends, the way in which it ends is what is most intriguing. Who of us did not weep when we read the last page of Shakespeare's *Hamlet?* Perhaps it ends as it does because each of us is Jonah today. Perhaps the Lord has shown you to yourself, warts and all, and you can complete the story.

> I've wandered far away from God,
> Now I'm coming home.
> The paths of sin too long I've trod,
> Lord, I'm coming home.
>
> I've wasted many precious years,
> Now I'm coming home.
> I now repent with bitter tears,
> Lord, I'm coming home.
>
> I'm tired of sin and straying, Lord.
> Now I'm coming home.
> I'll trust Thy love, believe Thy word,
> Lord, I'm coming home.
>
> My soul is sick, my heart is sore,
> Now I'm coming home.
> My strength renew, my hope restore,
> Lord, I'm coming home.

Did Jonah learn his lesson? I'm convinced he did. He didn't stop at the end of chapter 3 with the great revival, but he went on to show us himself "warts and all," and he let God have the last word.

1. Kendall, R. T. 1978. *Jonah.* London: Hodder & Stoughton, p. 234.
2. Blair, J. Allen. 1963. *Jonah.* Neptune NJ: Loizeaux Brothers, Inc., p. 167.
3. Kendall, *Jonah*, p. 250.